FAMILIES: RIGHTS, LAWS AND STABILITY

FAMILIES: RIGHTS, LAWS AND STABILITY

JANICE R. REDMUND
AND
KATHLEEN B. KILLIGAN
EDITORS

Nova Science Publishers, Inc.
New York

For permission to use material from this book please contact us:
Telephone 631-231-7269; Fax 631-231-8175
Web Site: http://www.novapublishers.com

LIBRARY OF CONGRESS CATALOGING-IN-PUBLICATION DATA

Families : rights, laws, and stability / Janice R. Redmund and Kathleen B. Killigan (editors).
p. cm.
ISBN 978-1-60456-203-3 (hardcover)
1. Domestic relations--United States. I. Redmund, Janice R. II. Killigan, Kathleen B.
KF505.F33 2007
346.7301'5--dc22

2007048143

Published by Nova Science Publishers, Inc. ✢ New York

CONTENTS

PREFACE

As populations in many developed countries begin to dwindle or become heavily unbalanced toward the aged, the support families, their structures and societal encouragement become vital issues. This new and important book examines some of the perplexing and complex issues involved in this battle for survival focusing on rights, laws and stability of the family.

Chapter 1 - Under the United States Constitution, Congress has little direct authority to legislate in the field of domestic relations. The primary authority and responsibility to legislate in the domestic relations arena lies with the individual states. The rationale behind this approach is the lack of overriding national considerations in the family law area. However, states' freedom to legislate has led to substantial variation between the individual states on many topics including incidents of marriage, divorce and child welfare. As such, Congress continues to utilize a number of indirect approaches to enact numerous federal laws which impact on family law questions. This article discusses the extent to which Congress is constitutionally authorized to legislate on family law questions, and includes examples of present laws utilizing the various approaches available in this area.

Chapter 2 - The tax provisions in the individual income tax have shifted over time, first in increasing the burden on larger families, and then in decreasing it. These shifts have been caused by changing features of the tax code: personal exemptions, standard and itemized deductions, rate structures, the earned income credit, the child credit, and other standard structural aspects of the tax. The distribution of tax burden across income classes has, however, changed relatively little, although burdens at the top and bottom have decreased in recent years.

While several standards may be considered in determining equitable treatment of families over family type and size, a standard approach is based on ability to pay, so that large families with the same income as small ones pay less tax. Based on this standard, the analysis of equity across families suggests that families with children are paying lower rates of tax (or receiving larger negative tax rates) than single individuals and married couples at lower and middle incomes. However, families with children are being taxed more heavily at higher income levels. At the lowest income levels, the EIC provides the largest tax subsidies to families with two or three children. The smallest subsidies go to childless couples. At middle income levels, families with many children will have the most favorable treatment, due to the effect of the child credit, which has a very large effect relative to tax liability. At higher income levels, large families are penalized because the adjustments for children such as personal exemptions and child credits are too small or are phased out, while graduated rates cause larger families that need more income to maintain a given living standard to pay higher taxes. Tax rates are more variable at lower income levels. At all but the lowest and very highest income levels, singles pay higher taxes than married couples.

The analysis of the marriage penalty indicates that marriage penalties have largely been eliminated for those without children throughout the middle income range, but this change has inevitably expanded marriage bonuses. Marriage penalties remain at the high and low income levels and could also apply to those with children, where the penalty or bonus is not very well defined. But by and large, the current system is likely to encourage rather than discourage marriage and favors married couples over singles.

The analysis of equity across families suggests that increases in earned income tax credits for those without children would lead to more equal treatment based on the ability to pay approach, while full refundability of the child credit would exacerbate inequalities. At the higher end of the scale, eliminating phaseouts of provisions that differentiate across families would probably lead to more equitable treatment, and containing the effect of the alternative minimum tax is important to both reducing the high burden of taxes on families with children at upper middle income levels as well as preventing an increasing level of marriage penalties.

Chapter 3 - In 2005, 23% of families with children were maintained by mothers. According to some estimates, 60% of children born during the 1990s will spend a significant portion of their childhood in a home without their father. Research indicates that children raised in single-parent families are more likely than children raised in two-parent families (with both biological parents) to do poorly in school, have emotional and behavioral problems, become teenage parents, and have poverty-level incomes. In hopes of improving the long-term outlook for children in single-parent families, federal, state, and local governments, along with public and private organizations, are supporting programs and activities that promote the financial and personal responsibility of noncustodial fathers to their children and increase the participation of fathers in the lives of their children. These programs have come to be known as "responsible fatherhood" programs.

Sources of federal funding for fatherhood programs include the Temporary Assistance for Needy Families (TANF) program, TANF state Maintenance-of-Effort (MOE) funding, welfare-to-work funds, Child Support Enforcement (CSE) funds, and Social Services Block Grant (Title XX) funds.

Beginning with the 106th Congress, the House but not the Senate passed bills containing specific funding for responsible fatherhood initiatives (in the 107th and 108th Congresses as part of welfare reauthorization bills). Moreover, from the start President Bush has been a supporter of responsible fatherhood programs; each of his budgets has included funding for such programs. In the 109th Congress, P.L. 109-171 — the Deficit Reduction Act of 2005 — was enacted. It included a provision that provides up to $50 million per year (FY2006-FY2010) in competitive grants to states, territories, Indian tribes and tribal organizations, and public and nonprofit community groups (including religious organizations) for responsible fatherhood initiatives.

Most fatherhood programs include media campaigns that emphasize the importance of emotional, physical, psychological, and financial connections of fathers to their children. Most fatherhood programs include parenting education; responsible decision-making; mediation services for both parents; providing an understanding of the CSE program; conflict resolution, coping with stress, and problem-solving skills; peer support; and job-training opportunities (skills development, interviewing skills, job search, job-retention skills, job-advancement skills, etc.). To help fathers and mothers meet their parental responsibilities, many policy analysts and observers support broad-based collaborative strategies that go beyond welfare and child support agencies and include schools, work programs, prison systems, churches, community organizations, and the health care system.

The federal government's support of fatherhood initiatives raises a wide array of issues. This article briefly examines the role of the CSE agency in fatherhood programs, discusses initiatives to promote and support father-child interaction outside the framework of the father-mother relationship, and summarizes the debate over whether fatherhood programs should include the "promotion of marriage."

Chapter 4 - Since 1965, the U.S. government has supported international population planning based on principles of volunteerism and informed choice that gives participants access to information on all methods of birth control. This policy, however, has generated contentious debate for over two decades, resulting in frequent clarification and modification of U.S. international family planning programs. Given the divisive nature of this debate, U.S. funding of these programs will likely remain a point of contention during the 110th Congress.

In 1984, controversy arose over U.S. population aid policy when the Reagan Administration introduced restrictions, which became known as the "Mexico City policy." The Mexico City policy denies U.S. funds to foreign non-governmental organizations (NGOs) that perform or promote abortion as a method of family planning — even if the activities are undertaken with non-U.S. funds. Presidents Reagan and George H.W. Bush also banned grants to the U.N. Population Fund (UNFPA) due to evidence of coercive family planning practices in China.

President Clinton resumed UNFPA funding and reversed the Mexico City policy in 1993. President George W. Bush, however, re-applied the Mexico City restrictions. Following a State Department investigation of family planning programs in China, the Administration suspended U.S. contributions to UNFPA in 2002, citing violations of the "Kemp-Kasten" amendment, which bans U.S. assistance to organizations that support or participate in the management of coercive family planning programs. The suspension of U.S. contributions to UNFPA has continued through FY2007.

Foreign operations programs are currently being funded under the terms of a continuing resolution, which provides funding similar to the FY2006 level with some adjustments. Therefore, the current level of funding for bilateral family planning activities should be around $440 million — the enacted level for bilateral population assistance activities in FY2006 (see H.R. 3057/P.L. 109-102).

The Bush Administration's FY2008 budget request includes $324.8 million for family planning health activities. The Administration proposed that $25 million in UNFPA funding be drawn from the $324.8 million bilateral family planning request if the organization is determined eligible under the Kemp-Kasten amendment.

On June 21, 2007, the House passed H.R. 2764, the State, Foreign Operations, and Related Appropriations Bill, FY2008, which appropriates $441 million for reproductive health and voluntary family planning programs, and $40 million for UNFPA if it is found eligible under the Kemp-Kasten amendment. On June 22, 2007, the Senate passed its version of H.R. 2764, which appropriated $461.06 million for family planning and reproductive health programs. It did not specify a funding amount for UNFPA.

Chapter 5 - In 1993, Congress passed the Family and Medical Leave Act ("FMLA") to "balance the demands of the workplace with the needs of families." When the FMLA was enacted, it supplemented approximately 30 state statutes that provided some form of family and medical leave to employees who worked in those states. Although the FMLA and state family and medical leave laws are generally similar with regard to the availability of leave, they differ both in terms of coverage and scope. This article includes summaries of the family and medical leave laws of forty-five states and the District of Columbia. Laws pertaining to family and medical leave and maternity leave were not found in the codes of all 50 states. Summaries of the relevant leave statutes and regulations are organized in alphabetical order.

Chapter 6 - The Even Start program provides education and related services jointly to parents lacking a high school diploma (or equivalent) and their young children. Even Start services include basic academic instruction and parenting skills training for the adults, and early childhood education for their children, along with necessary supplementary services such as child care or transportation. Generally, Even Start programs do not directly provide all of these services; rather, they establish networks of service providers, including Head Start programs and grantees under the Adult Education Act (AEA). Even Start is the only federal program specifically dedicated to providing services to both disadvantaged young children and their parents.

The families served by Even Start programs are highly disadvantaged, with very low levels of education and income, and increasing proportions of them have limited English language skills.

The Even Start program was reauthorized in the 106th Congress, in P.L. 106-554, the Departments of Labor, Health and Human Services, Education, and Related Agencies Appropriations Act for FY2001. ESEA Title I, Part B was renamed the William F. Goodling Even Start Family Literacy Programs and was reauthorized for five years beginning with an authorization of $250 million for FY2001. The reauthorizing language is largely the same as language contained in the Literacy Involves Families Together Act, H.R. 3222 (Goodling), which was passed by the full House on September 12, 2000. However, language in H.R. 3222 specifying that religious organizations should be treated the same as other nongovernmental organizations in the awarding of subgrants *was not* included in the final reauthorization language.

P.L. 107-110 (the No Child Left Behind Act of 2001), the Elementary and Secondary Education Act reauthorization legislation, which was signed into law on January 8, 2002, moved the William F. Goodling Even Start Family Literacy Programs from Title I Part B of the ESEA to Subpart 3 of Title I Part B of the No Child Left Behind Act and extended the authorization period through FY2007. The only change to the program was an amendment allowing states to use funds for state-level activities to improve the quality of family literacy services provided (in addition to other previously authorized uses).

The Even Start program's funding was reduced to $99 million for FY2006 (including the FY2006 across-the-board reduction). For FY2007, the Administration has requested no funding for the program, the House Committee on Appropriations has recommended $70 million in funding for the program, and the Senate Committee on Appropriations has recommended no funding for the program.

Chapter 7 - Supplemental Security Income (SSI) is a major benefit program for low-income persons with disabilities and senior citizens. As a means tested program, SSI places income and resource limits on individuals and married couples for the purposes of determining their eligibility and level of benefits. To become and remain eligible to receive SSI benefits, single individuals may not have countable resources valued at more than $2,000 and married couples may not have countable resources valued at more than $3,000. Although a person's home and car are excluded from these calculations, most other assets owned by a person or married couple are counted and in most cases, the assets of both partners in a marriage are considered shared and equally available to both the husband and the wife.

A person's countable income must be below SSI program guidelines to qualify for benefits and a person's monthly benefit level is reduced by a portion of his or her earned and unearned income. The income of a person ineligible for SSI can be considered when calculating the benefit amount of that person's spouse. A complicated process of deeming is used to determine how much of the ineligible person's income is to be considered when calculating his or her spouse's monthly SSI benefits.

In some cases marriage may result in a person being denied SSI benefits or seeing his or her SSI benefit level reduced because of the increase in family income or assets that results from the marriage. This can occur if an SSI beneficiary marries another SSI beneficiary or a person not in the SSI program. This potential effect of marriage on the SSI eligibility and benefits of SSI beneficiaries has been called a "marriage penalty" by the National Council on Disability.

This article provides an overview of the potential effect of a marriage to another SSI recipient or an ineligible person on an individual's eligibility for and level of SSI benefits. Examples of cases in which a marriage can reduce a person's SSI benefits are provided. To date, no legislation has been introduced in the 110th Congress that would change the way marriage can affect SSI eligibility and benefits.

This article provides an overview of the potential effects of marriage on Supplemental Security Income (SSI) eligibility and benefits. It includes an overview of the SSI program, information on the SSI resource limits, and a discussion of how the marriage of an SSI beneficiary to either another beneficiary or an ineligible person can affect his or her eligibility for benefits or monthly benefit level. In some cases, marriage may result in a person being denied SSI benefits or having his or her monthly SSI benefit level reduced. This situation has been called a "marriage penalty" by the National Council on Disability.[1]

Chapter 8 - In 1978, Congress enacted the Indian Child Welfare Act (ICWA) in response to legislative findings of harm caused to Indian children, their families, and tribes by the high separation rate of Indian children from their homes and cultural environments. Congress addressed this situation by granting Indian tribes and Indian parents an enhanced role in determining when to remove Indian children from their homes and cultural environments. Specifically, the ICWA enumerates provisions for tribal jurisdiction and tribal intervention in state court proceedings concerning the custody, adoption, foster care placement, and termination of parental rights of Indian children.

No bills amending the ICWA were introduced in the 109th Congress. Still, the debate over provisions of the ICWA remains an issue of concern. This CRS report provides an overview of some of the goals and provisions of the Indian Child Welfare Act.

In: Families: Rights, Laws and Stability
Editors: J. R. Redmund, K. B. Killigan, pp. 1-27
ISBN: 978-1-60456-203-3

Chapter 1

FAMILY LAW: CONGRESS'S AUTHORITY TO LEGISLATE ON DOMESTIC RELATIONS QUESTIONS*

Alison M. Smith

ABSTRACT

Under the United States Constitution, Congress has little direct authority to legislate in the field of domestic relations. The primary authority and responsibility to legislate in the domestic relations arena lies with the individual states. The rationale behind this approach is the lack of overriding national considerations in the family law area. However, states' freedom to legislate has led to substantial variation between the individual states on many topics including incidents of marriage, divorce and child welfare. As such, Congress continues to utilize a number of indirect approaches to enact numerous federal laws which impact on family law questions. This article discusses the extent to which Congress is constitutionally authorized to legislate on family law questions, and includes examples of present laws utilizing the various approaches available in this area.

Under the United States Constitution,[1] Congress has little direct authority to legislate in the field of domestic relations. Generally, state policy guides these decisions. Despite the lack of direct authority to legislate domestic relations issues, Congress continues to utilize a number of indirect approaches to enact numerous federal laws which impact on family law questions.

The Constitution's framers felt that states, rather than the federal government, should maintain jurisdiction over most family law questions. Thus, the final document reflects that view. As summarized by the Supreme Court in *Hisquierdo v. Hisquierdo*, 439 U.S. 572, 581 (1979):

* Excerpted from CRS Report RL31201, dated October 19, 2006.

> Insofar as marriage is within temporal control, the States lay on the guiding hand. "The whole subject of the domestic relations of husband and wife, parent and child, belongs to the laws of the States and not to the laws of the United States." In *re Burrus*, 136 U.S. 586, 593-94 (1890)...On the rare occasion when state family law has come into conflict with a federal statute, this Court has limited review under the Supremacy Clause to a determination whether Congress has "positively required by direct enactment" that state law shall be preempted. *Wetmore v. Markoe*, 196 U.S. 68, 77 (1904).

Thus, the individual states have the primary authority and responsibility to legislate in the domestic relations arena, which includes incidents of marriage, divorce, and child welfare. The rationale behind this approach is the lack of overriding national considerations in the family law area. Therefore, states generally have the freedom to legislate as they see fit on these questions. However, states' freedom to legislate has led to substantial variation between the individual states on many of these topics, although more uniformity now exists than at any time in the past.[2] Thus, similarly situated spouses, parents and children may have different legal options depending on where they reside. For example, the community property concept of marital property adopted by nine states[3] is quite different from the common law property system in the other forty-one states. While all states have some form of no-fault divorce, based either on grounds such as "irreconcilable differences" or some period of separation, many authorize divorces based on fault or consider marital fault as a factor when awarding spousal support or dividing marital property. In addition, states have varying rules regarding the "who, what, when and where" of marriages and/or divorces.

Adoption is another area in which states have diverse regulations. Individual states have different statutes regarding the rights of adopted adults, birth parents, adoptive parents, birth siblings and birth relatives to gain access to identifying[4] and non-identifying[5] information about the adoptee or birth relatives. For example, a few states permit adoptees to gain access to their birth and/or adoption records,[6] but most require a court order issued for "good cause" (usually a medical crisis or some comparably serious situation) before unsealing such information. Although many states use similar procedures, the laws and processes surrounding access in any one state are unique.

During the first half of the twentieth century, numerous constitutional amendments were proposed which, if adopted would have authorized Congress to enact uniform national marriage and divorce laws. However, none of these proposals received the requisite two-thirds vote of each House of Congress necessitating submission to the states for ratification.[7] This approach now appears disfavored[8], in part due to a continuing view that the federal government should refrain from intervening in most family matters and in part because other approaches (all discussed *infra*) have led, or have the potential of leading, toward the same result in those areas where uniformity is thought desirable.

For example, the National Conference of Commissioners on Uniform State Laws (NCCUSL), a non-governmental entity, has proposed uniform laws on a number of family law topics, many of which have been widely adopted by the states. A more expansive view of congressional power to legislate under its commerce clause authority has led to federal legislation such as the Parental Kidnapping Prevention Act (PKPA), which authorizes federal intervention into certain custodial interference cases where applicable state law classifies such action as a felony. Also, Congress has enacted legislation under the Full Faith and Credit Clause. Legislation under this clause directs sister states to give full faith and credit to child custody, child support and protection orders of other states. Congress passed the Defense of

Marriage Act, which permits sister states to give no effect to the law of other states with respect to governing same-sex marriages. Congress has also established a number of funding programs whereby states must comply with detailed requirements in such areas as child abuse and the adoption of hard-to-place children before they can receive federal money to help deal with these problems.

This article discusses the extent to which Congress is constitutionally authorized to legislate on family law questions, and includes examples of present laws utilizing the various approaches available in this area.

GENERAL CONSTITUTIONAL PRINCIPLES

There are generally applicable constitutional principles which limit the authority of all governmental entities (federal, state, and local) to legislate on family law questions. The Fourteenth Amendment's Due Process Clause[9] has a substantive component which "provides heightened protection against government interference with certain fundamental rights and liberty interests,"[10] including parents' fundamental rights to make decisions concerning the care, custody, and control of their children.[11] Although the Constitution fails to mention specifically a fundamental right to privacy, courts recognize this right to encompass contraception, abortion, marriage, procreation, education (elementary level) and interpersonal relations.[12] These aspects broadly termed "private family life" are constitutionally protected against government interference. As such, a governmental entity must demonstrate a compelling interest to regulate or infringe on an individual's fundamental right. As summarized by the Supreme Court in *Moore v. City of East Cleveland*, 431 U.S. 494, 499 (1977):

> "This Court has long recognized that freedom of personal choice in matters of marriage and family life is one of the liberties protected by the Due Process Clause of the Fourteenth Amendment." *Cleveland Board of Education v. LaFleur*, 414 U.S. 632, 639-40 (1974). A host of cases, tracing their lineage to *Meyer v. Nebraska*, 262 U.S. 300, 399-401 (1923), and *Pierce v. Society of Sisters*, 268 U.S. 510, 534-35 (1925), have consistently acknowledged a "private realm of family life which the state cannot enter." *Prince v. Massachusetts*, 321 U.S. 158, 166 (1944).

The *LaFleur* decision struck down various local maternity leave rules which required pregnant teachers to begin leave at specified stages of their pregnancies and not to return to work until some specified point in the school year after their children were born or attained a certain age. *Meyer* and *Pierce* invalidated statutes which were held to interfere with parents' right to educate their children as they see fit; the *Meyer* statute prohibited instruction in foreign languages before the eighth grade,[13] while the statute in *Pierce* required children to attend public schools.[14] *Moore* stuck down a local ordinance that specified which members of extended families could reside together in common households — in the particular household which formed the basis for the suit, two grandchildren could have legally resided with their grandmother under the ordinance were they siblings, but were prohibited from doing so because they were first cousins.[15]

While "the family is not beyond regulation," *Prince v. Massachusetts, supra* at 166 (ban on street selling by minors upheld), "when government intrudes [into family matters], this Court must examine carefully the importance of the governmental interests advanced and the extent to which they are served by the challenged regulations." *Moore, supra,* at 499.

In *Griswold v. Connecticut,*[16] the Supreme Court recognized an additional tenet of privacy: the right of married couples to use contraceptives. The Court extended this right to minors, married or unmarried, in *Carey v. Population Services International.[17]* Also, In *Roe v. Wade,*[18] the Supreme Court substantially limited governmental authority to regulate abortions, holding that a mother's personal privacy right prevented a state from intervening at the first trimester of pregnancy, and permitted intervention during the second trimester only as needed to protect the mother's health. The Court reasoned that a state's interest fails to become compelling enough to justify extensive regulation until a fetus becomes viable, at approximately the end of the second trimester. This ruling was clarified, but retained in three companion cases decided in 1983: *Akron Center for Reproductive Health, Inc. v. City of Akron[19]*; *Planned Parenthood Association of Kansas City, Missouri, Inc. v. Ashcroft;[20]* and *Simopoulous v. Virginia.[21]* In 1992, the Supreme Court reaffirmed *Roe's* essential holding that before viability of the fetus, a woman has the right to choose to have an abortion and has the right to obtain an abortion without undue interference from the state.[22] In *Planned Parenthood of S.E. PA v. Casey,* the Court held that a statute requiring spousal notification before a woman could have an abortion constituted an undue burden, thus violating the due process clause of the Fourteenth Amendment.[23] However, the remaining four challenged aspects of the Pennsylvania Abortion Control Act of 1982 were found to be constitutional and not undue burdens. The Court held valid: (1) the act's definition of a "medical emergency," a condition warranting exemption from the act's other limitations; (2) record keeping and reporting requirements imposed on facilities that perform abortions; (3) an informed consent and 24-hour waiting period requirement; and (4) a parental consent requirement, with the possibility for a judicial bypass.[24]

A right to marry has also been judicially accepted as a guarantee of due process. Thus, the Court struck down miscegenation statutes in *Loving v. Virginia,[25]* finding that the state lacked a compelling interest in prohibiting persons from marrying based solely on their race.

The equal protection clause[26] is another constitutional limitation on governmental entities' authority to legislate on domestic relations issues. When legislation or government policy discriminates between classes or deprives a group of a particular right, the level of scrutiny applied under an equal protection challenge turns on the nature of the group allegedly discriminated against. As a general rule, courts will uphold the challenged governmental action if the classification drawn by the statute is rationally related to a legitimate state interest.[27] For example, states can legislate to protect minors, prevent close relatives from marrying, require blood tests before marriage and impose other marriage restrictions so long as the restrictions are reasonably related to a valid state interest.

Where the statute targets a quasi-suspect class, namely those based upon gender or illegitimacy, a heightened level of scrutiny applies. Under this intermediate scrutiny test, the statute is presumed invalid unless it is substantially related to a sufficiently important governmental interest.[28] For example, in *Orr v. Orr,*[29] the Supreme Court applied this standard and found a statute which imposed alimony obligations on husbands, but not on wives unconstitutional as violative of the equal protection clause. However, where a statute targets a suspect class, including race, alienage, or national origin or burdens a fundamental right, the statute in question will only be sustained if it is narrowly tailored to serve a compelling state interest. Under this standard, the Court has stuck down statutes in *Eisenstadt v. Baird[30]* and *Skinner v. Oklahoma[31]* as violative of the equal protection clause. Conversely, in *Nguyen v. INS*,[32] the Supreme Court found a statute which provided different rules for attainment of citizenship depending upon whether the one citizen parent was the father or mother, did not violate the equal protection clause.[33]

One instance where these arguments have been unsuccessful involves adult adoptees seeking to obtain information on their birth parents. Such adoptees have advanced both personal privacy and equal protection claims when challenging closed records statutes. However, courts consistently ruled that the privacy rights of the birth parents, as well as the state's interest in maintaining a smoothly-functioning adoption system (parents might become reluctant to place children for adoption if they thought the children would later seek them out), justify these laws.[34] However, the Supreme Court has yet to rule on this question so the issue of closed records statutes remains unsettled.

THE ENUMERATED POWERS CLAUSE

As opposed to the general constitutional restraints discussed above, Article I, Section 8, of the Constitution, the enumerated powers clause, limits congressional authority to act by specifying general subject categories where federal action is permissible. These categories encompass those topics the Constitution's framers thought could best be handled on the national level, such as war-making and defense, interstate and foreign commerce, coinage and currency, the post office, bankruptcies, copyrights, and the judicial system. Under this clause and the Tenth Amendment,[35] categories other than those enumerated are reserved for state action.

These enumerated powers do not readily encompass most family law questions. As such, federal legislation in this area is usually hinged on some other federal interest. For example, while states have the primary authority to legislate on adoption, alien children less than sixteen years of age adopted by unmarried United States citizens have been granted immigrant status.[36] Legislation such as the Indian Child Welfare Act[37] is based on congressional authority over Indian questions. States retain general authority over child pornography, but the federal government can regulate that portion which moves in interstate or foreign commerce, and/or which is shipped through the mail.[38]

Where Congress has authority to act in a given area, it can exercise one of three options: Congress can (1) supersede all state action on the question; (2) defer entirely to individual state judgments; or (3) legislate somewhere between these two extremes. Congress's options can best be illustrated by looking at its handling of former spouses' entitlements to pensions paid under a federal retirement program. Under Social Security and the Railroad Retirement System,[39] a former spouse who meets specified conditions is entitled to 50% of the covered spouse's benefit,[40] while federal civil service and military pensions are divisible at the option of the individual state hearing the matter (i.e., states are authorized to treat civil service[41] and military retirement[42] payments the same way they treat other pensions for this purpose). The acts governing foreign service and Central Intelligence Agency pension division[43] are hybrids between these two approaches, as they suggest a pro rata division formula predicated on length of marriage/length of service, but permit deviation from this formula by court order or if the parties agree to some other arrangement.

Where congressional intent is unclear or ambiguous, as was the case pertaining to the possible division of military pensions in divorce cases for some time,[44] or where Congress fails to act in a certain area when it has the authority to do so, individual states are free to act and/or interpret the applicable federal statutes as they see fit, subject to the constitutional considerations discussed above. However, once Congress acts to clarify its intent, states are bound by this interpretation and are no longer free to vary their approaches.

Overview of Federal Domestic Relations Legislation

Areas in which Congress Has Direct Authority to Legislate

Federal Benefits

Congress has plenary legislative authority over federal salaries, pensions, and other benefits, including those aspects which touch on family law questions. The State of California advanced a strong argument in *McCarty v. McCarty*, 453 U.S. 210 (1981), (where the court ultimately held federal law prevented state division of military pensions in divorce cases), that its interest in its residents' well-being, along with general state authority over divorce law, was sufficient to confer upon its courts the authority to grant a divorced wife a share of her husband's military pension. The Supreme Court disagreed, citing congressional power under Article I, Section 8, Clause 14 of the Constitution "[t]o make Rules for the Government and Regulation of the land and naval Forces." The military system was enacted pursuant to this grant of constitutional authority, and the Court found that the application of state community property law as envisioned by the lower court *McCarty* rulings (which divided the pension) could potentially frustrate the congressional objectives of providing for retired personnel and meeting the management needs of the active forces. However, the *McCarty* court recognized the serious plight of an ex-spouse of a retired service member,[45] and invited Congress to change the situation legislatively if so desired. Congress shortly thereafter enacted the Uniformed Services Former Spouses' Protection Act (FSPA),[46] which authorized states to divide, or not divide, these pensions in accordance with applicable state laws and precedents.

As discussed in the preceding section, Congress has for the most part deferred to state judgments in those divorce cases which involve pensions paid to federal employees. Of the pertinent statutes, only the Foreign Service Act and the CIA retirement Act contain suggested division formulas. These optional formulas take into account the particularly disadvantageous economic position of many of the wives whose husbands served in the Foreign Service or with the CIA. Under the Social Security Program, a former spouse who was married to an annuitant spouse with ten or more years of covered service[47] is entitled to 50% of the annuitant's pension at the time he or she reaches age 62, provided the former spouse has not remarried prior to that time.[48] This is a separate entitlement which does not reduce or affect the annuitant spouse's payment. Even in the absence of these statutes, voluntary division of annuities was possible if the parties so agreed. However, as might be imagined, such action occurred infrequently.[49]

Certain former spouses of Social Security,[50] Civil Service,[51] military,[52] railroad,[53] CIA,[54] and Foreign Service[55] annuitants are entitled to survivor annuities (annuities which continue after the annuitant spouse's death). Moreover, federal payments, including wages, pensions, tax refunds, and most other benefits, can be garnished for alimony and child support payments.[56]

Taxation

Nearly every tax imposed by Congress has at least a tangential impact on family life, if only because it determines how much money the family might have available to it under specified circumstances. This topic is much too complex to provide more than a brief overview of possibly relevant provisions and approaches.

Congress frequently uses its taxing power to establish social policies, as shown in its determinations that people should be encouraged to adopt,[57] to contribute to charitable organizations,[58] or purchase their own homes.[59] To promote marriage neutrality,[60] Congress passed the Economic Growth and Tax Relief Reconciliation Act of 2001.[61] Another tax provision frequently thought to have major social policy implication involves tax deductions for certain child care expenditures.[62] However, these deductions may show congressional recognition that both parents often must work for financial reasons, or there is only one parent to support the family, rather than a congressional belief that both parents should necessarily be encouraged to work outside the home.

Furthermore, there are numerous tax provisions which become operable when couples divorce. Frequently those negotiating a financial settlement can choose among several options which can have a substantial impact on the amount of money available to each spouse following the divorce. Tax laws treat child support and alimony differently. For example, alimony or separate maintenance payments from one spouse to another are deductible by the person making the payments and treated as taxable income to the recipient, while child support payments are neither taxable income to the recipient nor deductible by the payer.[63]

There are also a number of tax laws which reference adoption. For the most part, these statutes provide that adopted children are to be treated the same as natural born children for whatever purpose is involved.[64]

Bankruptcy

Article I, Section 8, Clause 4 of the Constitution authorizes Congress to establish "uniform Laws on the subject of Bankruptcies throughout the United States." As with taxation, the entire Bankruptcy Code, codified as Title 11 of the United States Code, can have an effect on the family lives of those involved in personal or business-related bankruptcies. However, for family law purposes, the most important provision prohibits individuals from discharging alimony and/or child support payments.[65] Other provisions may affect such situations as the timing of a bankruptcy petition *vis a vis* the filing of a divorce suit, or interspousal transfers prior to the filing of a bankruptcy petition or while such a petition is pending.

Indians

Generally, Indian tribes have extensive power to regulate domestic relations among tribal members. As summarized in the authoritative text on this subject:

> Indian tribes have been accorded the widest possible latitude in regulating the domestic relations of their members. Indian custom marriage has been specifically recognized by federal statute, so far as such recognition is necessary for purposes of inheritance. Indian custom marriage and divorce has been generally recognized by state and federal courts for all other purpose....No law of the state controls the domestic relations of Indians living in tribal relationship, even though the Indians concerned are citizens of the state...Property relations of husband and wife, or parent and child, are likewise governed by tribal law and custom.[66]

However, some tribes specifically defer to state authority in this area,[67] recognizing as valid marriages and divorces where pertinent state statutes have been followed. Federal law[68] permits states to assume jurisdiction over civil causes of action between Indians or to which Indians are parties, and which arise in Indian country, as long as the tribe occupying the particular Indian country specifically consents to the exercise of jurisdiction.[69] Once the tribe consents, this authority encompasses such civil actions as marriage, divorce, and adoption.[70]

These various approaches are recognized under 25 U.S.C. § 372a which states that "heirs by adoption" for purposes of certain probate matters shall include adoptions entered by a state court or an Indian court; those approved by the superintendent of the agency having jurisdiction over the tribe of either the adoptee or the adoptive parent; and adoptions handled in accordance with procedures established by the tribal authority of the tribe of either the adoptee or the adoptive parent. Rights of parties to marriages between Indians and non-Indians are set forth at 25 U.S.C. § 181-184.

The Indian Child Welfare Act (ICWA)[71] is a comprehensive measure designed to "protect the best interests of Indian children and to promote the stability and security of Indian tribes and families."[72] Establishment of minimal federal standards for the removal of Indian children from their homes and procedures for their foster or adoptive placement, and funding a variety of Indian child and family welfare programs help facilitate the act's goals. Indian tribes retain jurisdiction over custody proceedings involving Indian children unless they specifically decline to exercise it.[73]

Upon attaining age 18, Indian adoptees are entitled to receive information as to their birth parents' tribal affiliation and other information necessary to protect rights flowing from their tribal relations.[74] This is the only federal statute dealing with the confidentiality of adoption records.

Indirect Approaches

Congress utilizes indirect approaches in instances where it lacks direct authority to legislate in the domestic relations field. These indirect approaches include (1) the Commerce Clause; (2) a funding nexus or spending power; (3) Uniform State laws; (4) "Sense of Congress" resolutions; and (5) the Full, Faith and Credit Clause of the Constitution.

The Commerce Clause

Article I, Section 8, Clause 4 of the Constitution authorizes Congress "to regulate Commerce with foreign Nations, and among the several States." There are three categories of activities subject to congressional regulation under the Commerce clause. Congress may regulate the use of the channels of interstate commerce, or persons or things in interstate commerce, although the threat may come only from intrastate activities. Finally, Congress may regulate those activities having a substantial relation to interstate commerce.[75] Thus, Congress can regulate interstate aspects of certain family law matters even in the absence of direct legislative authority in the area.

For example, the Federal Parent Locator Service, an office in the Department of Health and Human Services (HHS) helps states locate non-custodial parents who fail to make court-ordered child support payments, once states have exhausted their own efforts to locate these individuals.[76] Under the Parental Kidnapping Prevention Act of 1980 (PKPA),[77] this office also acts on requests from authorized persons to locate non-custodial parents who have abducted their children from custodial parents in violation of valid court orders.[78]

The PKPA also makes the Federal Fugitive Felon Act[79] applicable to cases involving parental kidnapping and interstate or international flight to avoid prosecution under applicable state felony statutes. This provision again defers to state judgments inasmuch as the provision fails to become operable unless the state where the violation occurred has classified such action as a felony.

A parent whose child has been taken out of the country has greater difficulty in locating the child and arranging for his or her return than if the child remains in this country.[80] However, if the taking is classified as a felony, extradition treaties can sometimes be used to effectuate this result. The Hague Conference on Private International Law completed work on a Convention on the Civil Aspects of International Child Abduction, which the Senate consented to October 9, 1986. Congress adopted legislation to clarify how the Convention would be implemented in this country.[81]

The Commerce Clause also serves as the basis for federal regulation of child pornography that moves in interstate or foreign commerce.[82]

In 1992, Congress passed the Child Support Recovery Act (CSRA)[83] which created a federal criminal offense for any willful[84] failure to pay past child support obligations to a child who resides in a different state than the parent.[85] Appellate courts that have thus far heard appeals of the CSRA decisions have unanimously declared the CSRA a constitutional exercise of congressional authority, pursuant to the Commerce Clause.[86] The Second Circuit pointed to the fact that various state courts attempted to make the defendant pay his child support, but failed.[87] Because the Commerce Clause gives Congress the authority to pass legislation which aids the states in matters that are beyond their "limited territorial jurisdiction,"[88] the court concluded that Congress has the authority to intervene and help the states.[89] Further, it held that if Congress can use the Commerce Clause to promote interstate commerce, then "it surely has power to prevent the frustration of an obligation to engage in commerce."[90] Merely because the obligation comes from a court order, and not a contract, does not alter the outcome; the obligation is, nevertheless, a result of interstate economic activity among the states.[91] The Supreme Court has yet to rule on this question.

Funding Nexus

The public child welfare system is society's mechanism for protecting children whose families are unsafe or unable to care for them. States have the primary responsibility for administering child welfare services and establishing policy. However, the federal government plays a significant role in child welfare, by providing funds to states and attaching conditions to these funds. Provision of these funds is a valid exercise of Congress's spending power as Article 1, Section 8 of the Constitution authorizes Congress to use federal monies to provide for the common defense and the general welfare. These programs have been judged not to violate the Constitution due to the voluntary nature of states' participation. States and localities remain free to reject the federal monies; but if accepted, they are taken subject to the conditions imposed by Congress.

Most federal funds specifically targeted toward child welfare activities flow to the states through the Social Security Act, which authorizes capped grants for various child welfare services (Subparts 1 and 2 of Title IV-B), and open-ended entitlement funding for foster care maintenance and adoption assistance on behalf of children removed from their biological homes (Title IV-E). In addition, the freestanding Child Abuse Prevention and Treatment Act (CAPTA) authorizes formula grants to help states support their child protective services systems.[92] As such, the Federal Child Abuse Prevention and Treatment Act[93] imposes detailed requirements on state participants, including, *inter alia*, implementation of state programs which mandate the reporting of known or suspected instances of child abuse or neglect; investigation of such reports by properly constituted authorities; the provision of protective and treatment services to endangered children; immunity provisions for persons making good-faith reports of suspected instances of abuse and neglect; confidentiality of records, with criminal sanctions for those who illegally disseminate protected information; cooperation between agencies dealing with child abuse and neglect cases;[94] and other topics which would assist in identifying, preventing and treating child abuse and neglect.[95] This law is not aimed at those guilty of the abuse; but, rather is intended to help discover, treat and prevent as many child abuse cases as possible.

In the case of the Federal Child Support Enforcement Program (CSE),[96] the federal nexuses are the federal matching funds obtained by the states. All fifty states, the District of Columbia, Guam, Puerto Rico, and the Virgin Islands operate CSE programs and they are entitled to the matching federal funds. This program provides seven major services on behalf of children: (1) parent location, (2) paternity establishment, (3) establishment of child support orders, (4) review and modifications of support orders, (5) collection of support payments, (6) distribution of support payments and establishment and enforcement of medical support.[97]

To provide these services to children, requirements are put upon the states and participants alike. State requirements include automated registries of child support orders along with a centralized automated state collection and disbursement unit. Likewise, applicants and recipients are required to cooperate in establishing paternity or obtaining support payments or risk penalties for noncompliance. If a determination is made that an individual is uncooperative without any good cause or other exception, then the state must reduce the family's benefit by at least 25% and may even remove the family from the program.

Collection methods used by CSE agencies include income withholding, intercepts of federal and state income tax refunds, intercepts of unemployment compensation, liens against property, security bonds, and reporting child support obligations to credit bureaus. Moreover, all jurisdictions have civil or criminal contempt-of-court procedures and criminal non-support laws. Public Law No. 105-187, the Deadbeat Parents Punishment Act of 1998, established two new federal criminal offenses (subject to a two-year maximum prison term) with respect to non-custodial parents who repeatedly fail to financially support children who reside with custodial parents in another state or who flee across state lines to avoid supporting them.[98] Furthermore, P.L. 104-193, officially known as the Personal Responsibility and Work Reconciliation Act of 1996, required states to implement expedited procedures to allow them to secure assets to satisfy arrearages by intercepting or seizing periodic or lump sum payments (such as unemployment and worker's compensation), lottery winning, awards, judgments, or settlements, and assets of the debtor parent held by public or private retirement funds, and financial institutions.[99] In addition, the law required states to implement procedures under which the state would have authority to withhold, suspend or restrict use of driver's licenses, professional and occupational licenses, and recreational and sporting licenses of persons who owe past-due support or who fail to comply with subpoenas or warrants relating to paternity or child support proceedings.[100]

Uniform State Laws

The National Conference of Commissioners on Uniform State Laws is a non-governmental entity formed in 1982 "to promote uniformity in state laws on all subjects where uniformity is deemed desirable and practical."[101] Since the entity's inception, it has drafted and approved several uniform acts, which have met with varying degrees of success in terms of enactment by state legislatures. Three uniform domestic relations acts which have gained widespread acceptance deal with the enforcement of child support orders (UIFSA) and recognition of child custody decrees (UCCJEA and UCCJA) entered in other states. All states adopted the Uniform Interstate Family Support Act (UIFSA) under which state courts basically treat valid child support orders entered in another state as having been entered in their own state (the state which has jurisdiction over the person required to pay the support) for enforcement purposes.[102] The states' adoption of the UIFSA was due to Congress's enactment of welfare reform, officially known as the Personal Responsibility and Work Opportunity Reconciliation Act of 1996.[103] In this act, Congress mandated enactment of UIFSA for a state to remain eligible for the federal funding of child support enforcement.[104]

UIFSA provides procedural and jurisdictional rules for essentially three types of interstate[105] child support proceedings: (1) a proceeding to establish a child support order; (2) a proceeding to enforce a child support order and (3) a proceeding to modify a child support order. UIFSA implements the "one-order system." This means that only one state's order governs, at any given time, an obligor's support obligation to any child. Further, only one state has continuing jurisdiction to modify a child support order. This requires all other states to recognize the order and to refrain from modifying it unless the first state has lost jurisdiction.

UIFSA only governs jurisdiction to hear interstate child support proceedings. The Uniform Child Custody Jurisdiction Act (UCCJA)[106] (or the Uniform Child Custody Jurisdiction and Enforcement Act [UCCJEA])[107] and the Parental Kidnapping Prevention Act (PKPA)[108] govern jurisdiction to hear custody proceedings.

Thus, the forwarding of a UIFSA proceeding to a state that would not normally have jurisdiction over custody issues[109] does not subject the petitioner to custody claims the respondent might make. Further, a court properly hearing a UIFSA proceeding "may not condition the payment of a support order issued under (UIFSA) upon compliance by a party with provisions for visitation."[110]

One would think that a final domestic relations decree entered in one state should be uniformly recognized and enforced throughout the other states. However, this was frequently not the case, because in many instances a second state would assert its own jurisdiction to modify the original decree or enter a new decree which in its view supersedes the original one.[111] That is why, for example, the UCCJA, as discussed above, failed, despite its widespread adoption by the states, to result in the broad national recognition of child custody decrees its sponsors anticipated and desired. Rather, non-custodial parents would take the child to another state, and that state, by virtue of its jurisdiction over the party seeking the modification, would enter a new decree changing the custody arrangement because circumstances changed since the entering of the original decree.[112] This meant that the child's mother could have a valid decree in one state, granting her custody, while the father had an equally valid decree in another state, granting him custody — with concomitant frustration and expenditures of time and/or money by both parents, yielding unfortunate results to the child. The Parental Kidnapping Prevention Act of 1980 (PKPA)[113] has now largely taken care of the problem.

However, it must be noted that the PKPA does not confer jurisdiction on the federal courts. This act merely delineates which jurisdiction may modify child support and custody orders. As such, the PKPA is inapplicable to instate disputes and only relevant in interstate disputes when the jurisdictions have conflicting laws. Under the Supremacy Clause, the jurisdictional guidelines set forth in the PKPA supersede any conflicting state law. As such, parents are bound by state court decisions regarding custody, visitation and support.

"Uniform acts" such as UIFSA, UCCJA, UCCJEA fail to specify what court orders must contain or what courts must consider when drafting them, but deal exclusively with their enforcement once finalized. Other proposals, such as the Uniform Marriage and Divorce Act (UMDA) and the Uniform Adoption Act, include specific guidelines for courts to follow in drafting these various orders.

Even when domestic relations laws are drafted with great specificity, they fail to yield comparable results in seemingly comparable cases. Each domestic relations case presents a unique fact pattern which gives judges and hearing examiners wide discretion in determining an equitable ruling in each case. Thus, it is difficult, if not impossible to talk in terms of "average" alimony awards or predict with any degree of accuracy what custodial arrangement a judge will order in a particular divorce case. Generally, a party who receives an adverse ruling can only appeal on an "abuse of discretion" ground, an extremely difficult standard to meet. For this reason, reported domestic relations cases[114] have little precedential value except when cited for general policy considerations. However, courts can modify alimony, child support and/or child custody (not marital property division)[115] provisions, upon a showing of changed circumstances.

Adoption of uniformed laws such as UIFSA, UCCJEA and UCCJA has aided in fostering consistency and efficiency in the enforcement of interstate child support and custody orders.

"Sense of the Congress" Resolutions

Another indirect approach which Congress utilizes to obtain desired results are "Sense of the Congress" resolutions. These resolutions lack any legally binding force or effect, but are introduced in the hope that if Congress goes on record as favoring a certain policy, the individual states will be encouraged to adopt legislation advancing that policy.

For example, H.Con.Res. 67 expressed the sense of the Congress that:

> [A] uniform State act should be developed and adopted which provides grandparents with adequate rights to petition State courts for privileges to visit their grandchildren following the dissolution because of divorce, separation, or death of the marriage of such grandchildren's parents, and for other purposes.

This resolution passed the House of Representatives on April 22, 1985 and passed the Senate on September 29, 1986.[116] Consequently, some states have enacted specific grandparent visitation statutes, while others include grandparents within a broader third-party visitation statute.

The content of these visitation laws varies greatly.[117] Several states limit visitation to cases involving deceased parents.[118] Others specifically extend the right to cases of divorce, annulment or separation. A few states allow grandparent visitation even over the objections of both parents in an ongoing family,[119] and even against the argument that parents have the constitutional right to raise their child as they see fit.[120] Most states, however, hold by statute or court decision that the ongoing family is not subject to enforced intrusion by grandparents, if both parents are fit and object.[121]

Implementation of the Full Faith and Credit Clause

Article, Section 1 of the Constitution, the Full Faith and Credit Clause, states:

> "Full Faith and Credit shall be given in each state to the public Acts, Records, and judicial proceedings of every other state. And the Congress may by general laws prescribe the manner in which such Acts, Records, and Proceedings shall be proved, and the effect thereof."

This clause applies principally to the interstate recognition and enforcement of judgments. It is settled law that final judgments are entitled to full faith and credit, regardless of other states' public policies,[122] provided the issuing state had jurisdiction over the parties and the subject matter.[123] Judgments subject to future modification, such as child support and child custody orders, are not considered final. Therefore, they are not entitled to full faith and credit.[124] As discussed below, however, Congress enacted the PKPA and the Full Faith and Credit for Child Support Act to accord full faith and credit to child custody and support orders.[125] The Full Faith and Credit Clause has rarely been used by courts to validate marriages because marriages are not "legal judgments." However, courts routinely recognize out-of-state-marriages.

Questions concerning the validity of an out-of-state marriage are generally resolved without reference to the Full Faith and Credit Clause. As previously discussed, marriages are not regarded as judgments. In the legal sense, marriage is a "civil contract" created by the States which establishes certain duties and confers certain benefits.[126] Validly entering the contract creates the marital status; the duties and benefits attached by a State are incidents of that status.[127]

The general rule of validation for marriage is to look to the law of the place where the marriage was celebrated, *lex celebrationis*. A marriage satisfying the contracting state's requirements will usually be held valid everywhere.[128] Many states provide by statute that a marriage validly contracted elsewhere is valid within the state. At least twenty-three states have adopted language substantially similar to the Uniform Marriage and Divorce Act (UMDA),[129] which states: "All marriages contracted...outside this State, that were valid at the time of the contract or subsequently validated by the laws of the place in which they were contracted...are valid in this State."[130] Several states provide an exception to this general rule by declaring out-of-state marriages void if against the state's public policy or if entered into with the intent to evade the law of the state. As such, eleven states have passed legislation prohibiting recognition of out-of-state same-sex marriage.[131] Moreover, Congress passed the Defense of Marriage Act (DOMA),[132] which prohibits the federal recognition of same-sex marriages and allows individual states to refuse to recognize such marriages performed or recognized in other states.[133]

The Full Faith and Credit clause is applicable to divorces. In two related cases known as *Williams I* [134] and *Williams II*, [135] the Supreme Court articulated the extent to which the Full Faith and Credit Clause applies in divorce cases. Both cases arose out of the following scenario: a man and a woman, both domiciliaries (permanent residents) of North Carolina and married to other people, moved to Nevada. They lived there for six weeks to satisfy the Nevada durational residency requirement for divorce, at which time they obtained divorces upon substituted service (i.e. their spouses were notified by publication only and failed to participate in the proceedings), married each other, and returned to North Carolina. North Carolina then began prosecution under its bigamous cohabitation statute.

In *Williams I*, the Supreme Court held that in granting the divorce, Nevada was justified in assuming that the parties were bona fide Nevada domiciliaries (a jurisdictional requirement). Thus, the divorce was valid and warranted recognition as such by the other states including North Carolina. However, in *Williams II*, the Court held that a divorce decree issued in one state could be collaterally impeached in another by proof that the court which tendered the decree lacked jurisdiction. In this particular case, the fact that the new Mr. and Mrs. Williams returned to North Carolina immediately following their marriage was sufficient to justify the North Carolina court's conclusion that the couple was not domiciled in Nevada at the time their divorce was granted. As such, the divorce was void because the issuing court lacked proper jurisdiction.

In *Williams II*, the rule remains in effect today, as modified by the Supreme Court's holding in *Sherrer v. Sherrer*, 334 U.S. 343 (1948), that a divorce cannot be subsequently attacked by a spouse for lack of jurisdiction if the spouse participated in the divorce proceeding and the divorce court specifically ruled that it had jurisdiction.[136] Under this ruling, if both parties participate in a divorce proceeding and/or consent to the court's jurisdiction (i.e., obtain a "bilateral" divorce, neither party can attack the decree for lack of jurisdiction).[137]

Due to the increased uniformity of divorce laws, states' adoption of no-fault divorce statutes and shorter durational residency requirements situations such as the ones mentioned above continue to decrease. These reasons reduce a party's need to seek out what may be viewed as a more favorable divorce jurisdiction. While the situation has minimized with domestic divorce decrees, a comparable situation now exists regarding certain foreign divorce decrees (e.g., those where only one party appears briefly in the issuing jurisdiction).[138]

The Full Faith and Credit Clause does not govern the domestic validity of divorce judgments from foreign countries. The rule of comity, which generally provides for recognition of foreign decrees issued by courts of competent jurisdiction, governs. However, the jurisdictional tests applied are usually those of the United States,[139] rather than the divorcing country. As such, a divorce obtained in a foreign country will be invalid in the United States if neither spouse was domiciled in that country, even if domicile is not required for jurisdiction under its law. New York is the only state which recognizes bilateral foreign divorces (where both parties participate) even where its own jurisdictional requirements are not satisfied.[140] No state recognizes such unilateral divorces (where only one party appears).

Justice Frankfurter, in a concurring opinion in *Williams I*, noted that Congress had the authority under the Full Faith and Credit Clause to require national recognition of divorce decrees, but had not yet chosen to exercise such authority:

> ...[I]t is clearly settled that if a judgment is binding in the state where it was rendered, it is equally binding in every state. This rule of law was not created by the federal courts. It comes from the Constitution and the Act of May 26, 1790, c. 11, 1 Stat. 122. Congress has not exercised its power under the Full Faith and Credit Clause to meet the special problems raised by divorce decrees. There will be time enough to consider the scope of its power in this regard when Congress chooses to exercise it. 317 U.S. at 306.

In response to this dicta, Senator Pat McCarran introduced bills in the 80th through the 83rd Congresses[141] which, if enacted would have required all states to recognize divorce decrees where: (1) the decree was final as to the issue of divorce; (2) the decree was valid in the state where rendered; (3) the decree stated that the jurisdictional prerequisites of the issuing stated had been met; and (4) the issuing state was the last state where the spouses were domiciled together as husband and wife; or the defendant was personally subject to jurisdiction in that state, or appeared generally in the divorce proceedings. The only exceptions included fraud of the successful party which misled the defeated party. Two of these bills passed the Senate, in 1952 and 1953,[142] but neither became law and no such measure is presently pending.

Congressional action under the Full Faith and Credit Clause has been minimal, "[i]ndeed, there are few clauses of the Constitution, the merely literal possibilities of which have been so little developed as the full faith and credit clause."[143] Only on five occasions has Congress enacted legislation to require States to give full faith and credit to certain types of acts, records and proceedings. Three of the enactments pertain to family law concerns.

To date, the major legislative initiative in this area is 28 U.S.C. § 1738A, a provision of the PKPA which requires states to give full faith and credit to child custody decrees entered in other states unless the state asked to modify the original order has jurisdiction to do so, and the state which issued the original order lacks jurisdiction to modify the order or declines to exercise its jurisdiction.[144] In addition, under 42 U.S.C. § 666(a), states must grant full faith and credit to each other's child support orders, to the extent of not modifying them retroactively.[145]

In 1994, the 103rd Congress passed the Full Faith and Credit for Child Support Orders Act,[146] requiring each state to enforce child support orders issued by the child's home state if done in compliance with the act's provisions. The law was designed so that a person with a valid child support order in one state would not have to obtain a second order in another state should the debtor parent move from the issuing court's jurisdiction. Rather, the second state must recognize the first state's order as valid, but can modify it only when the child and the custodial parent have moved to the state where the modification is sought or have agreed to the modification. Retroactive modification is prohibited, and prospective modification is authorized if the court finds that circumstances exist which justify a change.[147]

Also in 1994, Congress passed the Safe Homes for Women Act of 1994,[148] requiring states to recognize domestic violence protection orders issued by sister states. Any protection order issued by one state or tribe shall be treated and enforced as if it were an order of the enforcing state. The act extends to permanent, temporary, and ex parte protection orders. Full faith and credit is afforded during the period of time in which the order remains valid in the issuing state. Protection orders are only afforded full faith and credit if the due process requirements of the issuing state were met.

In the previous instances, Congress's exercise of its full faith and credit enforcement power was necessitated by the failure of sister state courts to give full faith and credit to orders not regarded as final judgments. Congress directed sister states to give full faith and credit to child custody, child support, and protection orders from other states. In effect, Congress required each state to give the child custody, child support, and protection orders of other states the same faith and credit it gives its own such orders.

Conversely, in 1996, Congress passed the Defense of Marriage Act (DOMA).[149] This act differs in one critical aspect from the other legislative enactments passed by Congress under its full faith and credit power: the DOMA permits sister states to give no effect to the law of other states.[150] Congress enacted DOMA in response to claims by advocates of same-sex marriage that, if any state legalizes same-sex marriage, all states and federal agencies will have to recognize as valid all same-sex marriages performed in that same-sex-marriage-permitting state.[151] Congress recognized that the legalization of same-sex marriage in any jurisdiction would have far-reaching potential effects upon all people and upon a wide spectrum of laws in the jurisdiction, ranging from marriage law to public school curricula, from custody law to public finances, from adoption to insurance issues, from alimony and property division to employment regulations.[152] Moreover, these potential effects involved a policy issue of great importance to the people of each jurisdiction warranting decision by each jurisdiction.

Proposed Constitutional Amendments

Between 1917 and 2001, 33 constitutional amendments were proposed to give Congress authority to legislate on marriage and divorce questions.[153] In addition, 12 bills were introduced during this period to provide for uniform marriage and divorce laws throughout the United States, presumably in anticipation that such a constitutional amendment would be ratified.[154]

Eleven of the proposed constitutional amendments[155] and all of the implementing bills introduced in the Senate were sponsored by Senator Arthur Caper. The text of his proposed amendments uniformly stated:

> The Congress shall have power to make laws, which shall be uniform throughout the United States, on marriage and divorce, the legitimization of children, and the care and custody of children affected by annulment of marriage or by divorce.

However, none of these proposed amendments ever received congressional action. Beginning in the 107th Congress, legislation has been introduced proposing a constitutional to define marriage as the "union of a man and a woman."[156]

Conclusion

In the absence of a constitutional amendment providing general authority for Congress to legislate in the field of domestic relations, its direct authority is limited to those areas specifically reserved for congressional action under Article I, Section 8, of the Constitution. However, various indirect approaches, most notably those tied to congressional authority under the commerce clause and Congress's appropriations powers, have resulted in significant federal impact on a myriad of family law questions.

Currently, there appears to be little sentiment in favor of a national marriage and divorce law, at least one which would be imposed involuntarily by Congress on the states. However, it is probable that federal involvement will continue or be forthcoming in those areas where it is argued that federal resources can be utilized more efficiently and effectively than those available at the state or local level, such as tracking down parental kidnappers or establishing and enforcing child support orders. The spending power can be used to shape state approaches to a given situation, although this option involves expenditures of federal funds; the higher the funding level, the more likely a state is to comply with the federal directive.

The nature of family law cases is such that an individualized approach to each particular case will undoubtedly continue. However, state domestic relations laws have become more uniform in recent years, and even without federal intervention this trend is likely to continue. Thus, it is possible that some of the national uniformity envisioned by proponents of adopting a constitutional amendment for this purpose will be realized, although states retain primary authority to legislate in this area.

References

[1] U.S. Const. art. VI, § , cl. 2 states "This Constitution, and the Laws of the United States which shall be made in Pursuance thereof;...shall be the supreme Law of the Land; and the Judges in every State shall be bound thereby, any Thing in the Constitution or Laws of any State to the Contrary notwithstanding." However, this language encompasses only those areas where Congress has authority to legislate; *see* discussion of the enumerated powers clause, *infra*.

[2] For example, all states adopted the Uniform Interstate Family Support Act (UIFSA) under which states treat valid child support orders entered in another state as having been entered in their own state. States' adoption of uniformed laws such as UIFSA, Uniform Child Custody Jurisdiction Act (UCCJA) and the Uniform Child Custody Jurisdiction and Enforcement Act (UCCJEA) have aided in fostering consistency and efficiency in the enforcement of interstate child support and custody orders.

[3] Arizona, California, Idaho, Louisiana, Nevada, New Mexico, Texas, Washington and Wisconsin (due to statutory changes initiated in 1986).

[4] Identifying information encompasses data which may lead to positively identifying an adopted adult, birth mother, or birth father such as names, addresses, and dates contained in court records or submitted to the State Department of Vital Statistics.

[5] Non-identifying information is generally restricted to details about the adopted adult and the adopted adult's birth relatives. Information can include any of the following: date and place of adopted adult's birth; age of the birth parents and a description of their general physical appearances; the race, ethnicity, religion, and medical history of the birth parents; type of termination; facts and circumstances relating to the adoptive placement; age and sex of children of the birth parents at the time of adoption; educational levels of the birth parents and their occupations, interests, skills; any supplemental information about the medical or social conditions of members of the birth family provided since the adoption's completion.

[6] Adopted adults 18 or older have automatic access to their original birth certificates only in Alaska, Kansas, and, in some cases Ohio, Tennessee, and Montana, depending upon which year the adoption was finalized.

[7] Article V of the U.S. Constitution provides two ways to propose amendments to the document and two ways to ratify them. Amendments may be proposed either by the Congress, by two-thirds vote of the House and the Senate (of those present and voting, provided a quorum is present), or by a convention called by Congress in response to applications from the legislatures of two-thirds (34) or more of the states.

[8] However, beginning in the 107th Congress, legislation proposing a constitutional amendment defining as or limiting marriage to the "union of a man and a woman." See, H.J.Res. 93, 107th Cong.; H.J.Res. 56, S.J. Res. 26, and S.J. Res. 30, 108th Cong.; S.J. Res. 1, S.J. Res. 13, and H.J.Res. 39, 109th Cong.

[9] The Fourteenth Amendment forbids any State to "deprive any person of life, liberty, or property, without due process of law," or to "deny to any person within its jurisdiction the equal protection of the laws."

[10] *Washington v. Glucksberg*, 521 U.S. 702, 720 (1997).

[11] *Id.*; see also *Reno v. Flores*, 507 U.S. 292, 301-302 (1993).

[12] In addition to the specific freedoms protected by the Bill of Rights, the "liberty" specially protected by the Due Process Clause includes the rights to marry, *Loving v. Virginia*, 388 U.S. 1 (1967); to have children, *Skinner v. Oklahoma ex rel. Williamson*, 316 U.S. 535 (1942); to direct the education and upbringing of one's children, *Meyer v. Nebraska*, 262 U.S. 390 (1923); *Pierce v. Society of Sisters*, 268 U.S. 510 (1925); to marital privacy, *Griswold v. Connecticut*, 381 U.S. 479 (1965); to use contraception, ibid.; *Eisenstadt v. Baird*, 405 U.S. 438 (1972); to bodily integrity, *Rochin v. California*, 342 U.S. 165 (1952), and to abortion, *Planned Parenthood of Southeastern Pa. v. Casey*, 505 U.S. 833 (1992).

[13] *Meyer v. Nebraska*, 262 U.S. 300, 399-401 (1923).

[14] *Pierce v. Society of Sisters*, 268 U.S. 510, 534-35 (1925).

[15] *Moore v. City of East Cleveland*, 431 U.S. 494, 499 (1977).

[16] 381 U.S. 479 (1965).

[17] 431 U.S. 678 (1977).

[18] 410 U.S. 113 (1973).

[19] 462 U.S. 416 (1983).

[20] 462 U.S. 476 (1983).

[21] 462 U.S. 506 (1983).

[22] *Planned Parenthood of S.E. PA v. Casey*, 505 U.S. 833 (1992).

[23] *Id.*

[24] *Id.*

[25] 388 U.S. 1 (1967).

[26] The Fourteenth Amendment guarantees that "[n]o State shall make or enforce any law which shall deny to any person within its jurisdiction the equal protection of the laws." While there is no corresponding provision applicable to the federal government, the Fifth Amendment Due Process Clause applies the same limitation to the federal government.

[27] *See e.g., Romer v. Evans*, 517 U.S. 620 (1996) (applying the rational basis test in analyzing the equal protection challenge to the state constitutional amendment which prohibited all governmental action designed to protect homosexuals from discrimination).

[28] *See generally, United States v. Virginia*, 518 U.S. 515 (1996) (stating that if gender-based governmental discrimination is to pass judicial muster, the state must demonstrate the existence of an "exceeding persuasive justification.").

[29] 440 U.S. 268 (1979); *see also Califano v. Goldfarb*, 430 U.S. 199 (1977)(finding unconstitutional a statute which imposed a one-half support requirement on widowers, but not on widows, in establishing surviving spouse benefits' entitlements).

[30] 405 U.S. 438 (1972)(finding unconstitutional a Massachusetts statute prohibiting the distribution of contraceptives to unmarried persons).

[31] 316 U.S. 535 (1942)(holding a law requiring sterilization of certain criminals violative of equal protection; but emphasizing the importance of marriage and procreation).

[32] 533 U.S. 52 (2001).

[33] *Id.* The Court found that two important governmental interests justified Congress's decision to impose different requirements: (1) the importance of assuring a biological parent-child relationship exists; and (2) the determination ensuring that the child and citizen parent have some demonstrated "opportunity to develop a relationship that consists of real, everyday ties providing a connection between child and citizen parent." *Id.*

[34] *See*, e.g. *ALMA Society v. Mellon*, 601 F.2d 1125 (2d Cir. 1979); *Yesterday's Children v. Kennedy*, 569 F.2d 431 (7th Cir. 1979).

[35] The Tenth Amendment states, "The powers not delegated to the United States by the Constitution, nor prohibited by it to the States, are reserved to the States respectively, or to the people."

[36] 8 U.S.C. § 1101.

[37] P.L. 95-608, 92 Stat. 3069, codified at 25 U.S.C. §§ 1901-1963.

[38] 18 U.S.C. §§ 2251-2259,2423; 19 U.S.C. § 1305; See also, CRS Report 95-406 "*Child Pornography: Constitutional Principles and Federal Statutes*", by Henry Cohen.

[39] 42 U.S.C. § 402(b) (Social Security); 45 U.S.C. § 231a (Railroad Retirement). These payments do not reduce the retired spouses' entitlements.

[40] Many of the laws cited in this article have exceptions or technicalities not covered by these general summaries. The texts of the particular statutes should be consulted if additional information is required.

[41] 5 U.S.C § 8345(j)(1).

[42] 10 U.S.C. § 1408.

[43] 22 U.S.C. § 4044 (foreign service); § 222 of the Central Intelligence Agency Retirement Act, (CIARA) codified as a note following 50 U.S.C. § 403.

[44] Although there is no federal statute directly on point, the Supreme Court examined a number of related statutes and congressional documents before deciding in *McCarty v. McCarty*, 453 U.S. 210 (1981), that Congress had not intended that military pensions be divisible in this context. At the time of this decision, all of the community property states and a number of equitable distribution states were dividing military pensions, but they could no longer do so after it was issued. The *McCarty* decision and subsequent legislative action to authorize such division is discussed in the next section.

[45] 453 U.S. at 253.

[46] 10 U.S.C. § 1408.

[47] Periods of employment where the annuitant spouse paid into the Social Security System.

[48] 42 U.S.C. § 402(b).

[49] In the vast majority of divorce cases, the parties work out their financial arrangement without court assistance, and the court routinely incorporates this agreement as part of the final decree unless it is on its face grossly unfair to either party. Thus, there is no reason why an annuitant spouse cannot voluntarily agree to divide his or her annuity with the other spouse, presumably in return for some other consideration; and such agreements, once finalized by court order, are binding on the parties. However, the rationale behind legislatively sanctioning such division is that it is unlikely many annuitants will voluntarily agree to split a pension when there is no legal requirement to do so.

[50] 42 U.S.C. § 402(e), (f).

[51] 5 U.S.C. § 8341(h)(1).

[52] 10 U.S.C. § 1447.

[53] 45 U.S.C. § 231a.

[54] CIARA, § 204, codified as a note following 50 U.S.C. § 403.

[55] 22 U.S.C. § 4054.

[56] 42 U.S.C. §§ 659-662, 664

[57] P.L. 107-16, 115 Stat. 38 extends permanently the adoption credit for children other than special needs children. In addition, the act increases the maximum credit to $10,000 per eligible child, including special needs children. The act also extends permanently the exclusion from income for employer provided adoption assistance.

[58] 26 U.S.C. § 170 (deductions to qualified organizations tax exempt).

[59] 26 U.S.C. § 163 (mortgage interest tax exempt).

[60] Marriage neutrality means that the tax system should not influence the choice of individuals with regard to their marital status. For a discussion on the marriage tax penalty relief provisions of the Economic Growth and Tax Relief Reconciliation Act of 2001, see CRS Report RS21000, "*Marriage Tax Penalty Relief Provisions of the Economic Growth and Tax Relief Reconciliation Act of 2001*" by Gregg A. Esenwein.

[61] P.L. 107-16, 115 Stat. 38. This act contains three marriage tax penalty relief provisions: (1) increases the standard deduction for joint returns to twice the amount of the standard deduction for single returns; (2) increase the width of the 15% marginal income tax

bracket for joint returns to twice the width of the 15% tax bracket for single returns; and (3) increases the earned income credit phaseout start and end points for joint returns.

[62] 26 U.S.C. § 44.

[63] 26 U.S.C. §§ 71(a), 215.

[64] *See, e.g.*, 26 U.S.C. § 318 (constructive stock ownership); § 2613 (tax on generation skipping transfers).

[65] 11 U.S.C. § 523(a)(5).

[66] Cohen, *Handbook of Federal Indian Law* 137 (4th ed. 1954), (footnotes and citations omitted).

[67] E.g. *State ex rel. Iron Bear v. District Court of Fifteenth Judicial District in and for Roosevelt County*, 162 Mont. 335, 512 P.2d 1292 (1972) (Assiniboine-Sioux Tribes); *Bad Horse v. Bad Horse*, 163 Mont. 445, 517 P.2d 893 (1974) (Cheyenne Tribe).

[68] 25 U.S.C. § 1322.

[69] Id.; *Kennerly v. District court of Ninth Judicial District of Montana*, 400 U.S. 423 (1972); *Poitra v. Demarrias*, 502 F.2d 23 (8th Cir. 1974).

[70] E.g., *Nononka v. Hoskins*, 645 P.2d 507 (Okla. 1982); *United States ex rel. Cobell v. Cobell*, 503 F.2d 790 (9th Cir. 1974).

[71] P.L. 95-608, 92 Stat. 3069, codified at 25 U.S.C. §§ 1901-1963.

[72] 25 U.S.C. § 1902.

[73] 25 U.S.C. § 1911.

[74] 25 U.S.C. § 1917.

[75] *United States v. Lopez*, 514 U.S. 549, 558-559 (1995) (citations omitted).

[76] 42 U.S.C. § 653.

[77] 28 U.S.C. § 1738A.

[78] 18 U.S.C. § 663.

[79] 18 U.S.C. § 1073.

[80] See generally Westbrook, "LAW AND TREATY RESPONSES TO INTERNATIONAL CHILD ABDUCTIONS," 20 Va. J. of Int'l L. 149 (1981).

[81] 42 U.S.C. §§ 11601-11607. The Hague Convention fails to provide for the recognition and/or enforcement of foreign custody decrees; rather, it requires restoration of the custody status quo that existed before the abduction. Thus, it denies the abductor any legal advantage in the country to which the child has been taken as courts in that country are under a treaty obligation to return the child to the country from which the child was abducted without conducting any proceedings on the merits of the underlying custody claim(s). For a discussion and analysis of the Convention, see "AMERICAN AND INTERNATIONAL RESPONSES TO INTERNATIONAL CHILD ABDUCTIONS," 16 N.Y.U.J. Int'l L. and Pol. 415 (1984).

[82] 18 U.S.C. §§ 2251-2259; *See also* CRS Report 95-406, "*Child Pornography: Constitutional Principles and Federal Statutes*", by Henry Cohen.

[83] P.L. 102-521, 106 Stat. 3403 (codified at 18 U.S.C. § 228).

[84] The original bill created a presumption that any nonpayment of child support was intentional. See 138 Cong. Rec. S17131 (daily ed. Oct. 7, 1992)(statement of Sen. Kohl). The bill which was actually enacted provided that the government must prove a willful failure to pay. See id.

[85] See 18 U.S.C. § 228(a).

[86] *See United States v. Faasse,* 265 F.3d 475 (6th Cir. Mich. 2001)(finding that the CRSA did not usurp state enforcement, as the act merely reinforced state laws which states were unable to enforce on an interstate basis); *United States v. Lewko,* 269 F.3d 64 (1st Cir. N.H. 2001); *United States v. Benton,* 2001 U.S. App. LEXIS 17385 (4th Cir. S.C. Aug. 3, 2001); *United States v. Johnson,* 114 F.3d 476 (4th Cir. 1997); *United States v. Parker,* 108 F.3d 28 (3rd Cir. 1997)(finding that CSRA falls within the cope of congressional authority under the Commerce Clause as a valid regulation of activity having a substantial effect upon interstate commerce); *United States v. Bongiorno,* 106 F.3d 1027 (1st Cir. 1997)*; United States v. Bailey,* 115 F.3d 1222 (5th Cir. 1997); *United States v. Hampshire*, 95 F.3d 999 (10th Cir. 1996); *United States v. Mussari*, 95 F.3d 787 (9th Cir. 1996)(holding that Congress possesses the power, under the Commerce Clause, to punish willful violations of child support orders); *United States v. Sage*, 92 F.3d 101 (2d Cir. 1996).

[87] *See Sage*, 92 F.3d at 103.

[88] *Id.* at 105.

[89] *Id.*

[90] *Id.* at 105-106.

[91] *Id.* at 106.

[92] Child protective services include investigation of child abuse and neglect reports and removal of children from home if necessary for their protection. Child welfare services include various home-based services to strengthen and improve family functioning, other supportive services to maintain children in their own homes, financial support and services for children while they are in foster care, services to reunite children with their families if possible, and adoption assistance or other permanency planning services for children if family reunification is not feasible.

[93] 42 U.S.C. §§ 5101-5115.

[94] This situation can pose a particular problem due to the interests of law enforcement personnel who wish to prosecute offenders may run counter to those of social workers, who want to minimize the child's traumatic experience, and if possible, return him or her to the household at an early date. These goals are made more difficult if a member of the household is charged with abuse and/or the child is called upon to discuss the abuse with law enforcement officers or in court.

[95] See CRS Report RL31082, *Child Welfare Financing: Issues and Options*, by Karen Spar.

[96] 42 U.S.C. §§ 651-66.

[97] See CRS Report 97-408, *Child Support Enforcement: New Reforms and Potential Issues,* by Carmen Solomon-Fears.

[98] P.L. 105-187, 112 Stat. 618 amending 18 U.S.C. § 228.

[99] P.L. 104-193, 110 Stat. 2105.

[100] Also, passports may be denied, revoked or restricted for individuals certified by a state agency as owing more than $5,000 in past due support. 42 U.S.C. 652(k) and 22 C.F.R §§ 51.70(a)(8), 51.72(a) and 51.80(a)(2).

[101] National Conference of Commissioners on Uniform State Laws' Constitution, § 1.2.

[102] Unif. Interstate Family Support Act, 9 (pt. IB) U.L.A. 306 (1999). *See also* discussion of the Federal Child Support Enforcement Act *infra* at 148.

[103] 42 U.S.C. § 666.

[104] 42 U.S.C. § 666(f). *See Kansas v. United States*, 24 F.Supp.2d 1192 (D. Kan. 1998)(upholding Title III of the Personal Responsibility and Work Opportunity Reconciliation Act of 1996 and its requirement of states to pass UIFSA against the Spending Clause and Tenth Amendment challenges).

[105] The word "interstate" is used here to mean that one or both parents have left the state in which they were married or maintained a relationship.

[106] 9 (pt IB) U.L.A. 261 (1999). Before the adoption of the UCCJEA in 1997, all fifty states and the District of Columbia had adopted the UCCJA.

[107] The National Conference of Commissioners on Uniform State Laws adopted the UCCJEA in 1997 as a replacement for the UCCJA.

[108] 28 U.S.C. § 1738A (1994).

[109] Under the PKPA, the UCCJEA, and, to a lesser extent, the UCCJA, the child's home state is favored for jurisdiction over custody issue.

[110] UIFSA § 305(d), 9 (pt. IB) U.L.A. 306 (1999). See id. Prefatory Note, 9 (pt.IB) U.L.A. 241, Part II.B.2.b (1999) ("Visitation issues cannot be raised in child support proceedings."). See, e.g., *Office of Child Support Enforcement v. Clemmons*, 984 S.W.2d 837 (Ark. Ct. App. 1999).

[111] In addition, most custody decrees are not final for purposes of the full faith and credit clause, as the issuing state may modify. Thus, the doctrine of *res judicata*, which holds that upon a finally adjudication a matter cannot be reopened or collaterally attacked in the original state or elsewhere, fails to apply in child custody decrees. See, e.g. *Kovacs v. Brewer*, 356 U.S. 604 (1958); *Ford v. Ford*, 371 U.S. 187 (1962).

[112] In many instances the only change was the fact that the child was not living with the other parent and sufficient time elapsed so that the court in the new state felt the best decision was to assure this new continuity of care for the child.

[113] P.L. 96-611, §§ 6-10, 94 Stat. 3566,3567; codified at 28 U.S.C. § 1738A.

[114] The only cases available for research purposes are those appealed. The appeal results in a written decision reprinted in various court reporting services.

[115] Marital property settlements are usually only modified upon a showing of fraud or coercion at the time the settlement was approved by the parties or imposed by the court.

[116] 132 Cong. Rec. S26904 (daily ed. September 29, 1986).

[117] The following is a list of state statutes governing third-party visitation. Alabama (Ala. Code § 30-3-4); Alaska (Alaska Stat. §§25.20.060, 25.20.065); Arizona (Ariz Rev. Stat.Ann. §25-409); Arkansas (Ark.Stat. Ann. §§9-13-102 and 9-13-103); California (Cal. Fam. Code §§ 3102-3104); Colorado (Colo. Rev. Stat. §§ 19-1-117 and 19-1-117.5); Connecticut (Conn. Gen. Stat. §§ 46b-56(a), 46b-57, 46b-59 and 46b-129); Delaware (Del. Code. Ann. Tit. 10 § 1031(7)); Florida (Fla. Stat. § 752.01); Georgia (Ga. Code § 19-7-3); Hawaii (Hawaii Rev. Stat §§ 571-46(7) and 571.46.3); Idaho (Idaho Code § 32-719); Illinois (Ill. Rev. Stat. Ch. 750 and 5/607); Indiana (Ind. Code §§ 31-17-5-1 thru 31-17-5-2); Iowa (Iowa Code § 598.35); Kansas (Kan. Stat. Ann. §§ 60-1616 and 38-129); Kentucky (Ky. Rev. Stat. § 405.021); Louisiana (La. Rev. Stat. Civ Code Ancillaries § 9:344 and Children's Code § 1264); Maine (Me. Rev. Stat. Ann. Title 19-A §§ 1653(2)(B) and 1801 through 1805); Maryland (Md. Fam. Law Code § 9-102); Massachusetts (Mass. Gen. Laws Ann. § 119-39D); Michigan (Mich. Comp. Laws §§ 722.27(b), 722.27b and 722.26c); Minnesota (Minn. Stat. §§ 257.022, 257c.08 and 518.1752); Mississippi (Miss. Code. Ann. §§ 93-16-1 and 93-16-7); Missouri (Mo.

Rev. Stat. § 452.402); Montana (Mont. Code Ann. § 40-9-102); Nebraska (Neb. Rev. Stat. §§ 43-1801 thru 43-1803); Nevada (Nev. Rev. Stat. §§ 125A.330 and 125A.340); New Hampshire (N.H. Rev. Stat. Ann. §§ 458:17d); New Jersey (N.J. Rev. Stat. § 9:2-7.1); New Mexico (N.M. Stat. Ann. §§ 40-9-1 thru 40-9-4); New York (N.Y. Dom. Rel. Law §§ 71 thru 72 and 240(1)); North Carolina (N.C. Gen. Stat. § 40-13.2); North Dakota (N.D. Cent. Code § 14-09-05.1; Ohio (Ohio Rev. Code Ann. § 3109.051); Oklahoma (Okla. Stat. Tit. 10 § 5); Oregon (Or. Rev. Stat. § 109.119); Pennsylvania (Pa. Cons. Stat. Tit. 23 §§ 5311 thru 5314); Rhode Island (R.I. Gen. Laws §§ 15-5-24.1 thru 15-5-24.4); South Carolina (S.C. Code Ann. § 20-7-420(33)); South Dakota (S.D. Codified Laws Ann. §§ 25-4-52 thru 25-4-54, and 25-5-29 thru 25-5-34); Tennessee (Tenn. Code Ann. §§ 36-6- 302 thru 36-6-303); Texas (Tex. Fam. Code Ann. §§ 154.432 thru 153.434); Utah (Utah Code Ann. §§ 30-3-5-5(a) and 30-5-2); Vermont (Vt. Stat. Ann. Tit. 15 §§ 1011 thru 1016); Virginia (Va. Code §§ 20-124.1 thru 20-124.2); Washington (Wash. Rev. Code Ann. § 26.09.240); West Virginia (W. Va. Code Chapter 48, article 10); Wisconsin (Wis. Stat. Ann. § 767.245); Wyoming (Wyo. Stat. § 20-7-101).

[118] *See e.g. Hiller v. Fausey*, 904 A.2d 875 (PA 2006)(holding that application of state statute allowing visitation or partial custody to grandparents upon the death of a child's parent did not violate the father's due process right to direct the care, custody, and control of his child); *see also, In re estate of Thurgood*, No. 20040796, 2006 WL 2457822 (Utah Aug. 26, 2006)(finding that grandparent visitation statute did not unconstitutionally infringe upon a parent's right to the care, custody, and control of his or her children).

[119] *State ex rel. Brandon L. v. Moats*, 551 S.E.2d 674 (W. Va. 2001)(finding Grandparent Visitation Act does not violate parents' substantive due process right of liberty in connection with the care, custody, and control of children without undue interference from the state because the act requires an affirmative determination that visitation would not substantially interfere with the parent-child relationship and places the burden of proof on grandparents to show that visitation is in the child's best interest); *but see Troxel v. Granville*, 530 U.S. 57 (2000)(finding unconstitutional a Washington statute allowing "any person" to petition a court "at any time" to obtain visitation rights whenever visitation "may serve the best interests" of a child as applied to an order requiring a fit parent to allow her child's grandparents more extensive visitation than the parent wished).

[120] *Id.;Lily v. Lily*, 43 S.W.3d 703 (Tex. App. 2001)(finding Grandparent visitation statute did not violate due process on its face, as statute allowed only grandparents under particular circumstance to petition for visitation, and provided that it was in child's best interests).

[121] *See e.g. Troxel v. Granville,* 530 U.S. 57; *see also*, *Linder v. Linder*, No. 01-380, 2002 WL 723898, *1 (Ark. Apr. 25, 2002) (holding state's grandparent visitation law invalid as applied to an otherwise fit mother who rebuffed the visitation requests of her deceased husband's parents); *Wickham v. Byrne*, No. 92048, 2002 WL 595036, *1 (Ill. Apr. 4, 2002) (finding Illinois grandparent visitation law facially invalid because it places a fit parent on equal footing with the parent seeking visitation); *State ex rel. Brandon L. v. Moats*, 551 S.E. 2d 674 (W. Va. 2001).

[122] In *Fauntelroy v. Lum*, 210 U.S. 230 (1908) the Supreme Court required Mississippi to give full faith and credit to a Missouri judgment, even though the judgment was based upon a "futures" contract, a transaction which Mississippi had outlawed as against its public policy.

[123] *Restatement (Second) of Conflict of Laws* § 107.

[124] *Restatement (Second) of Conflict of Laws* § 109.

[125] 28 U.S.C. 1738A.

[126] On the state level, common examples of nonnegotiable marital rights and obligations include distinct income tax filing status; public assistance such as health and welfare benefits; default rules concerning community property distribution and control; dower, curtesy and inheritance rights; child custody, support agreements; name change rights; spouse and marital communications privileges in legal proceedings; and the right to bring wrongful death, and certain other, legal actions.

[127] On the federal level, marriage results in: distinct housing entitlements; federal income tax rates; Medicare, Medicaid, and veterans' benefits; and immigration and citizenship rights.

[128] See, Annotation, 71 A.L.R. 687 (1960).

[129] Arizona, Arkansas, California, Colorado, Connecticut, the District of Columbia, Georgia, Hawaii, Idaho, Illinois, Kansas, Kentucky, Louisiana, Michigan, Minnesota, Montana, Nebraska, New Mexico, North Dakota, South Dakota, Utah, Virginia, Wyoming.

[130] Unif. Marriage and Divorce Act § 210, 9A U.L.A. 147.

[131] Alaska, Arizona, Georgia, Idaho, Illinois, Kansas, Oklahoma, South Carolina, South Dakota, Tennessee, Utah. For a discussion of same-sex marriages, refer to CRS Report RL31994, *Same-Sex Marriages* by Alison M. Smith.

[132] P.L. 104-199, 110 Stat. 2419, codified at 28 U.S.C. § 1738C.

[133] Id. Legislation was introduced in the 108th Congress to repeal the provisions of DOMA codified in Title 1. H.R. 2677, the "State Regulation of Marriage is Appropriate Act," was introduced by Congressman Barney Frank on July 9, 2003. The bill was referred to the House Committee on the Judiciary on July 9, 2003 and was referred to the Subcommittee on the Constitution on Sept. 4, 2003. No further action has been taken on this bill.

[134] *Williams v. North Carolina*, 317 U.S. 287 (1942).

[135] *Williams v. North Carolina*, 325 U.S. 226 (1945).

[136] When "[i]t is clear that respondent was afforded his day in court with respect to every issue involved in the litigation...there is nothing in the concept of due process which demands that a defendant be afforded a second opportunity to litigate the existence of jurisdictional fact." 334 U.S. at 348 (citations omitted).

[137] The Court further held in *Johnson v. Muelberger*, 340 U.S. 581(1951), that a child could not collaterally attack her parents' divorce where both parties participated in the proceeding.

[138] Such divorces are commonly known as "Mexican divorces," even though Mexico tightened its residency requirements in 1971 so that few American now qualify for a divorce in that country. However, several Caribbean countries continue this practice.

[139] State jurisdictional requirements ordinarily include some formal residency requirement (usually six months or a year) and proper notice to the opposing party.

[140] *Rosenstiel v. Rosenstiel*, 209 N.E.2d 709 (1965).

[141] S. 1960, 80th Cong., 2d Sess. (1948); S. 3, 81st Cong., 1st Sess. (1940); S. 1331, 82d Cong., 1st Sess. (1951); and S. 39,83d Cong., 1st Sess. (1953).

[142] S. 1331, 82d Cong., passed the Senate on June 21, 1952, 98 Cong. Rec. 7773; S. 39, 83d Cong., passed the Senate on May 6, 1953, 99 Cong. Rec. 4575.

[143] Constitution of the United States of America: Analysis and Interpretation 970 (1992).

[144] For specific jurisdictional requirements, see 28 U.S.C. § 1738A(c). Under this language, a state court retains jurisdiction over a child for six months after the child leaves the state, as long as the custodial parent continues to reside in that state.

[145] This provision was added as part of the Omnibus Budget Reconciliation Act of 1986, P.L. 99-509, Title X, § 9103(a), 100 Stat. 1973.

[146] P.L. 103-383, 108 Stat. 4064, codified at 28 U.S.C. § 1738B.

[147] 42 U.S.C. § 666(a).

[148] P.L. 103-322, title IV, § 40221(a), 108 Stat. 1930, codified at 18 U.S.C. § 2265.

[149] P.L. 104-199, 110 Stat. 2419, codified at 28 U.S.C. § 1738C.

[150] 28 U.S.C. § 1738C states: "No State, territory, or possession of the United States, or Indian tribe, shall be required to give effect to any public act, record, or judicial proceeding of any other State, territory, possession, or tribe respecting a relationship between persons of the same sex that is treated as a marriage under the laws of such other State, territory, possession, or tribe, or a right or claim arising from such relationship."

[151] The first step in this direction was taken by the Hawaii Supreme Court in *Baehr v. Levin*, 852 P.2d 44 (Haw. 1993). The *Baehr* court held that while there is no fundamental right for same-sex couples to marry, the state statute restricting marriage to opposite-sex couples established a sex-based classification subject to strict scrutiny for the purposes of an equal protection challenge. The court held that the statute amounted to sex discrimination when analyzed under this standard. Following this decision, the Hawaii state legislature amended the state constitution in 1998 to bar recognition of same-sex marriages and the state supreme court found that "the marriage amendment validated" the statute in question in *Baehr*.

[152] See H.R. Rep. No. 104-664, at 10-11 (1996)(discussing the interstate and federal implications of the legalization of same-sex marriages in any jurisdiction). In *Baker v. Vermont*, 744 A.2d 864 (Vt. 1999), the Vermont Supreme Court held that it was a violation of the state constitution to deny same-sex couples the benefits and protections afforded opposite-sex married couples. The plaintiffs in *Baker* were three same-sex couples in committed relationships ranging from four to twenty-five years; two of the couples had children they had raised as a family. The couples applied for marriage licenses and were rejected, and brought suit challenging the validity of the statute under which they were denied licenses. The trial court found in favor of the defendants, finding that limiting marriage to opposite-sex couples "rationally furthered the State's interest in promoting 'the link between procreation and child rearing.'" Recharacterizing the issue as one of equal protection, the Vermont Supreme Court held that same-sex couples must be afforded privileges and responsibilities under state law equal to those enjoyed by opposite-sex couples that are married. The holding does not mandate that same-sex couples be allowed to marry; instead, the Court left the exact procedure for effecting the change to the legislature. The Vermont state senate passed

the mandated bill in April 2000, allowing same-sex couples to form civil unions. While not labeled "marriages," these unions entitle the couples to all the state benefits of marriage.

[153] S.J.Res. 34, H.J.Res. 55, and H.J.Res. 187, 65th Cong., S.J.Res. 55, H.J.Res. 75, and H.J.Res. 108, 66th Cong.; S.J.Res. 31, S.J.Res. 273, H.J.Res. 83, and H.J.Res. 426, 67th Cong., S.J.Res. 5, S.J.Res. 53, H.J.Res. 6, H.J.Res. 9, H.J.Res. 40, and H.J.Res. 109, 68th Cong., S.J.Res. 31, H.J.Res. 30, H.J.Res. 58, and H.J.Res. 110, 69th Cong.; S.J.Res. 40, H.J.Res. 35, and H.J.Res. 162, 70th Cong.; S.J.Res. 123, 71st Cong.; S.J.Res. 234 and H.J.Res. 558, 7th Cong.; and S.J.Res. 28, 80th Cong.

[154] S. 4394 and H.R. 13976, 67th Cong.; S. 1751, 69th Cong.; S. 1707, 70th Cong.; S. 3147, 71st Cong.; S. 3098 and H.R. 8908, 75th Cong.; S. 791, 76th Cong.; S. 810, 77th Cong.; S. 460, 78th Cong.; S. 726, 79th Cong.; S. 198, 80th Cong.

[155] S.J.Res. 273, 67th Cong.; S.J. Res.5, 68th Cong.; S.J. Res.31, 69th Cong.; S.J.Res. 40, 70th Cong.; S.J.Res. 123, 71st Cong.; S.J.Res. 234, 75th Cong.; S.J.Res. 44, 76th Cong.; S.J.Res. 36, 77th Cong., S.J.Res. 24, 78th Cong.; S. J. Res. 47, 79th Cong.; and S.J.Res. 28, 80th Cong.

[156] H.J.Res. 93, 107th Cong.; H.J.Res. 56, S.J.Res. 26, and S.J. Res. 30, 108th Cong.; S.J.Res. 1, S.J.Res. 13, H.J.Res. 39, H.J.Res. 88, and H.J.Res. 91, 109th Cong.

In: Families: Rights, Laws and Stability
Editors: J. R. Redmund, K. B. Killigan, pp. 29-52
ISBN: 978-1-60456-203-3

Chapter 2

FEDERAL INCOME TAX TREATMENT OF THE FAMILY*

Jane G. Gravelle

ABSTRACT

The tax provisions in the individual income tax have shifted over time, first in increasing the burden on larger families, and then in decreasing it. These shifts have been caused by changing features of the tax code: personal exemptions, standard and itemized deductions, rate structures, the earned income credit, the child credit, and other standard structural aspects of the tax. The distribution of tax burden across income classes has, however, changed relatively little, although burdens at the top and bottom have decreased in recent years.

While several standards may be considered in determining equitable treatment of families over family type and size, a standard approach is based on ability to pay, so that large families with the same income as small ones pay less tax. Based on this standard, the analysis of equity across families suggests that families with children are paying lower rates of tax (or receiving larger negative tax rates) than single individuals and married couples at lower and middle incomes. However, families with children are being taxed more heavily at higher income levels. At the lowest income levels, the EIC provides the largest tax subsidies to families with two or three children. The smallest subsidies go to childless couples. At middle income levels, families with many children will have the most favorable treatment, due to the effect of the child credit, which has a very large effect relative to tax liability. At higher income levels, large families are penalized because the adjustments for children such as personal exemptions and child credits are too small or are phased out, while graduated rates cause larger families that need more income to maintain a given living standard to pay higher taxes. Tax rates are more variable at lower income levels. At all but the lowest and very highest income levels, singles pay higher taxes than married couples.

The analysis of the marriage penalty indicates that marriage penalties have largely been eliminated for those without children throughout the middle income range, but this change has inevitably expanded marriage bonuses. Marriage penalties remain at the high and low income levels and could also apply to those with children, where the penalty or

* Excerpted from CRS Report RL33755, dated December 19, 2006.

bonus is not very well defined. But by and large, the current system is likely to encourage rather than discourage marriage and favors married couples over singles.

The analysis of equity across families suggests that increases in earned income tax credits for those without children would lead to more equal treatment based on the ability to pay approach, while full refundability of the child credit would exacerbate inequalities. At the higher end of the scale, eliminating phaseouts of provisions that differentiate across families would probably lead to more equitable treatment, and containing the effect of the alternative minimum tax is important to both reducing the high burden of taxes on families with children at upper middle income levels as well as preventing an increasing level of marriage penalties.

Recent years have been times of significant changes in the income tax treatment of the family. For lower income families, the most important of these have been the expansion of the earned income credit (EIC) in 1990 and 1993. For middle income families, the introduction of the child credit in 1997 and its expansion in 2001-2003, along with the expansion of rate brackets and standard deductions to address the marriage penalty have been important features. For higher income families, the lowering of tax rates in general, and the increasing scope of the alternative minimum tax (AMT) are important changes.

While an array of issues might be considered in discussing tax rules and their effects, this paper considers two questions: what is an equitable treatment of families of different sizes, and what are the effects of marriage penalties and bonuses.

The first section summarizes the major features of the tax law affecting families and family choices, and how they developed over time, including the relatively recent introduction of large benefits for children at low and moderate income levels, a reversal of a trend in the past that tended to reduce these benefits through the erosion of the real value of the personal exemptions. It also summarizes the origin of the marriage penalty and marriage bonus.

The following two sections first discuss general equity issues, and then apply the ability-to-pay standard to examine how tax burdens vary by family size, across the income spectrum. The final section examines the marriage penalties and bonuses.

Development of Current Tax Treatment of the Family

Current federal income tax law differentiates among families by type and structure in several ways. This differentiation has changed considerably over the years and includes personal exemptions, standard deductions, rate schedules, and various other features such as child care credits, age exemptions, and earned-income credits.

Personal Exemptions; Child Credits

Personal exemptions allow a certain amount per person to be exempt from tax. Combined with standard deductions, which vary by family type, they exclude a minimum level of income from tax. In 1986, these combined amounts were roughly set at the poverty level. Personal exemptions can also play a part in marriage bonuses when only one spouse works: a single individual cannot claim an unmarried companion as a dependent, while a husband can claim a wife (and vice versa).

The tax laws have always allowed some relief for family size through exemptions, although the original 1913 act allowed deductions only for the individual taxpayer ($3,000) and spouse ($1,000). These amounts were very large relative to incomes, but the initial income tax was not intended to reach a broad group of individuals. Even when dependent exemptions were allowed in 1917, they were only $200, small relative to the basic exemptions. The practice of allowing an equal exemption for each family member began in the early 1940s.

Personal exemptions were reduced in the initial years of the tax, then increased, then reduced again; they were last reduced in the early 1940s. The real value of the exemptions was also affected by inflation. For example, the personal exemption remained constant at $600 from 1948 through 1969, while its real value was heavily eroded through inflation. It was gradually increased over the next ten years to $1,000, where it again remained constant until 1985. From 1948 through 1984 the personal exemption lost 63% of its purchasing power. In large part due to diminution of the real value of personal exemptions, the tax burden had shifted over time to fall more heavily on larger families.

In 1986 personal exemptions were increased and indexed, so that today the personal exemption has lost only about 24% of its purchasing power.[1] This shift of burden to families with children was changed dramatically by the adoption of the $500 child credits in the Taxpayer Relief Act of 1997 and by the increase in that credit to $1,000 in the Economic Growth and Recovery Act of 2001. In the cases where these credits apply (for children under 17), they caused the personal exemption plus the deduction equivalent of the credit to be 55% larger than its 1948 value with the $500 credit and 133% larger with the $1,000 credit for families in the 15% rate bracket; they are 23% and 70% larger respectively for families in the 25% bracket. The credit is not, however, indexed for inflation, and absent indexation its value will diminish. The $500 increase in the credit is to sunset in 2010 as well, although it may be extended or made permanent.

Not all taxpayers received the credit. It was phased out for higher incomes. The credit was not generally refundable and therefore families with no tax liability or insufficient liability to use the full credit would not receive the full benefit. An exception was made for families with three or more children where the credit could offset payroll tax in excess of the earned income tax credit.

When the child credit was doubled under the temporary provisions of the 2001 tax, an additional refundability provision was allowed for all families for income in excess of $10,000 (beginning at 10% and rising to 15%), indexed for inflation. The additional child credit was phased in initially, but accelerated in legislation adopted in 2003 and 2004.

The personal exemption is also phased out for higher incomes, although that phase-out is scheduled to expire.

Standard Deduction or Flat Exclusion; Itemized Deductions

Standard deductions, which vary across the types of returns (single, joint, and head of household), also affect tax burdens across families. Prior to the 2001 tax revision, the standard deductions for singles and heads of household were 60% and 80%, respectively, of the size of the deduction for joint returns. The standard deduction can contribute to a marriage penalty if it is larger than half the deduction for married couples: two singles who both work and marry will have a smaller combined deduction. It can also contribute to a marriage bonus, if there is only one earner in the couple, since the joint deduction is larger than the single deduction. In 2001, joint standard deductions were increased, so as to eliminate the marriage penalty relative to singles without children and reduce it relative to heads of household (where the deduction is 73% as large). These changes increased the marriage bonus.

Virtually from its inception, the tax law allowed deductions for taxes, interest, charitable contributions, and certain other personal expenses. In 1944, a standard deduction of 10% of adjusted gross income with a ceiling of $500 was allowed as a substitute for these itemized deductions.[2] A major reason for this exemption was to reduce the number of itemizers and make tax filing less complex. In 1964, a minimum standard deduction of $200 plus $100 for each exemption with a $1,000 ceiling was added. Beginning in 1969, these standard deductions were increased substantially. The percentage standard deduction was gradually increased to 16% and the ceiling increased to $2,000. A low-income allowance of $1,100, to be reduced by $50 in each of the next two years, was substituted for the minimum standard deduction. (These reductions were included because of the rise in the personal exemption that was increasing total exempt amounts). The low-income allowance was increased to $1,300 in 1972.

In 1975, the low-income allowance was once again differentiated, but based on family type (joint, head of household, single) rather than size. Joint returns received a $2,100 allowance by 1976. The ceiling on the percentage standard deduction was also differentiated by family type, and was raised to $2,800 for joint returns by 1976. In 1977, the low-income allowance and the percentage standard deduction were consolidated into a single flat allowance called the zero-bracket amount, which was set at $3,200 in 1977 and at $3,400 in 1978. This zero-bracket amount was indexed in 1981, so that it would rise with inflation. The Tax Reform Act of 1986 raised the flat deduction amount, but continued to differentiate it with respect to family status (but not family size). The 2001 act increased the standard deduction for joint returns to twice that of single returns.

In comparing the relative benefits over time, it is important to consider the changes in all flat allowances as well, not just the personal exemption. For example, while the real value of the personal exemption has declined about 24% since 1948, the exempt amount for a family of four (joint return) was very close to the exempt amount had 1948 values been indexed for inflation (using the GDP deflator) prior to the 2001 tax changes. Current levels are about 21% larger than those which would have occurred had the exempt level in 1948 been indexed.[3] Ignoring the child credit, smaller families have more generous exempt levels today, while larger ones have less generous levels. For example (again, ignoring the child credit), exempt allowances are larger in real terms today for singles (75% larger), for heads of households with one child or two children (46% and 20% larger respectively) and for joint returns with one to four children (39%, 31%, 11%, and 4% larger respectively). Real levels are about the same as 1948 for heads of household with four family members and smaller for those with more family members (1% for a five-person family, 6% for a six-person family). They are also smaller for joint-return families with five and six family members (2% and 5%, respectively).

Heads of household and joint returns with children eligible for the child credit, however, have greater exempt levels. For joint returns, assuming that additional members are eligible children, the credit causes all of them to have increased exempt amount equivalents between 87% and 117% higher than in 1948, with the larger increases for heads of households and large families with joint returns (whose values have tended to more than double).

Note, however, that changes in benefits compared to past levels do not necessarily have implications for the appropriate treatment of different families. If past family differentiation was not due to a theory about equitable treatment of differing families, there is no economic reason that current tax treatment should conform to any past standards.

Most taxpayers take the standard deduction but about a third itemize, largely at the higher income levels. Itemized deductions tend to keep pace with income levels. They are technically subject to a phase-out but the effect of the phase-out is to increase marginal tax rates, since it is triggered by income and not deductions.

Rate Structure

Two important aspects of the rate structure are the unit of taxation and the progressivity of the rate structure (that is, how tax rates rise as increments of income increase). Current tax rates are imposed at 10, 15, 25, 28, 33, and 35% under the provisions of the 2001 tax change; if those provisions expire the 10% rate will return to 15% and the top four rates will increase to 28, 31, 36, and 39.6%. Taxes are imposed on family units. Married couples cannot use the single rate schedules (although they can file separately with a rate structure that offers no advantage over joint filing). Most taxpayers have income that taxes them at no more than 10% (23% of returns), no more than 15% (41% of returns), and no more than 25% (15% of returns).[4]

The width of the brackets is greatest for joint returns and smallest for singles, although all types of returns reach the top 35% rate at the same point. For single returns the 10% and 15% brackets are half the width of joint returns, the 25% bracket is 70% as large, and the next two brackets are about 124% as large (longer brackets at the top being necessary to get to the same income for the top bracket). For heads of household the 10% and 15% brackets are 72% and 66% as wide, the next two about the same length and the final bracket 111% as wide.[5] There are also phase-outs of itemized deductions, personal exemptions, and child credits at very high income levels.[6] However, the higher rates and the phase-outs apply to only a small fraction of taxpayers. Less than 10% of taxpayers had adjusted gross income over $100,000 in 2003 and less than 2% had incomes over $200,000.[7]

In the original 1913 tax law, a single rate structure was applied to all taxpayers as individuals. In 1948, joint returns were allowed that effectively permitted income splitting. This change had little to do with any theory regarding the tax treatment of the family. Rather, it occurred because married couples in community property states were successfully claiming the right to divide their income evenly for tax purposes. Under a graduated rate structure, this income-splitting reduces the total tax burden by reducing the amount of income subject to higher rates. Income-splitting was adopted to equalize treatment across the states and to forestall a major tax-induced disruption in state property laws. This move created the familiar joint and single returns. Both the community property treatment and the legislated income-splitting resulted in a tax subsidy for marriage. Individuals who married would experience lower tax liabilities due to the rate structure as long as their incomes were unequal. Shortly after, in 1951, a head-of-household schedule for unmarried taxpayers with dependents was introduced which allowed half the benefits from income splitting (i.e., wider tax brackets). This treatment could, in theory, create a marriage penalty for families with children, although this point received virtually no attention.

Criticism from singles, arguing that their taxes were too high, led in 1969 to a singles rate schedule with wider brackets. This difference in rate schedules, however, also created a marriage penalty for certain types of families, including those without children. If both spouses worked, tax bills could increase with marriage. Many people were uncomfortable with a tax provision which encouraged couples to live together without benefit of matrimony. Coupled with increasing female labor force participation and a changing social structure, the marriage penalty created considerable concern. For this reason, a capped deduction for the secondary earner in a family was adopted in 1981. The provision allowed 10% of income to be deducted, subject to a cap of $3,000. This deduction was an imperfect device which partly alleviated the problem of the marriage penalty and, for individuals below the cap, reduced the marginal tax rate on the secondary worker. It was repealed in 1986, when the flatter rate structure caused the marriage penalty to be less severe. The marriage penalty was increased for very high income individuals in 1993 with the addition of higher tax rates. These changes affected, however, only a very small fraction of the population.

The degree of progression in the rate structure interacts to affect the tax burden that applies to taxpayers in different circumstances. The rate structure has varied significantly over time, but a major revision in the 1986 act reduced the brackets to two (15 and 28%) as well as lowering the top bracket. Certain benefits were phased out. In 1990, the "bubble" due to these phase-outs was eliminated in exchange for adding a new tax rate of 31%.[8] (Capital gains were held to a 28% rate). However, personal exemptions were still phased out. Itemized deductions were also phased out, on a temporary basis, reduced by 3% of adjusted gross income (AGI) above a limit. Since itemized deductions tend to rise with income faster than the reductions due to the phase-out, this phase-out is the equivalent of increasing taxable income by 3%, and an additional percentage point or so in tax. (Each dollar of adjusted gross income taxed leads to a reduction in deductions of $0.03, and if the marginal tax rate is around a third, then the additional tax per dollar of income is around $0.01). In 1993, two marginal tax rates were added at the upper income levels, 36% and 39.6%; this legislation made the itemized deduction and personal exemption phase-outs permanent.

The 2001 tax cut, in addition to lowering the top tax rates and introducing a new 10% rate, eliminated the marriage penalty for most taxpayers by increasing the standard deduction, new 10% rate bracket, and the 15% rate bracket to make these values twice as large as for singles, returning to the pre-1969 treatment for most taxpayers. That tax cut also prospectively eliminated the personal exemption phase out (to begin in 2006 and be complete in 2010) and the itemized deduction phase-out (in 2010).

Earned Income Tax Credit (EIC)

The earned income tax credit (EIC) is a refundable credit (or negative tax) that provides a wage subsidy for low-income working individuals. The credit is a percentage of earned income which reaches a maximum fixed amount and then is eventually phased out. The credit rates are currently 7.65% for families without children, 34% for families with one child, and 40% for families with two children. The phase-out levels are higher for families with children than for those without children. In 2005, the credit reached its maximum value of $399 for families with no children at an income of $5,220; the credit is phased out at incomes between $6,530 and $11,750 for singles and between $8,530 and $13,750 for joint returns. For families with one child, the maximum credit of $2,662 is reached at $7,830; the credit is phased out between $14,370 and $31,030 for single heads and between $16,370 and $33,030 for married couples. For families with two or more children, the maximum credit of $4,400 is reached at $11,000 and is phased out between $14,370 and $35,363 for single heads and between $16,3790 and $37,263 for married couples.

Unlike some other provisions, there is no differentiation by family type; rather, the differences depend on the presence of one, two or no children. The EIC plays a role in creating a marriage penalty for lower income families. If individuals with low earnings marry, the couple's higher combined income may phase out more of the earned income tax credit. At the same time, marriage can reduce taxes if a single individual marries someone with children but with little or no income, because he or she becomes eligible for the larger credit for families with children.

The earned income tax credit (EIC) was first enacted in 1975. This provision provided a refundable tax credit for 10% of earned income, phased out at a rate of 10% of income over $4,000. Because the credit was refundable, individuals who paid no income tax were nevertheless eligible for a benefit. There were a variety of rationales for the EIC: to provide a work incentive, to offset the social security tax burden, and to provide relief for recent price increases in food and fuel. The credit was, however, only allowed to individuals who maintained a household for dependent children; thus, like the major welfare program of the time, AFDC (Aid to Families with Dependent Children), the EIC as originally enacted was not extended to singles and childless couples.

The EIC has been revised in various ways, and in 1990 was differentiated with respect to number of children. In 1993, the credits were increased substantially and a small credit was added for families without children. The 2001 tax cut expanded the phase-out range for married couples which slightly reduced the marriage penalty in the EIC.

Child or Dependent Care Credit

Another provision allows for credits for paid child care expenses for children under 13 and disabled dependents. A deduction for these costs was first allowed in 1954 and converted to a credit in 1976. The credit is 30% of eligible expenses but is phased down to 20% as income rises from $15,000 to $43,000. Eligible expenses are limited to $3,000 for one child, and $6,000 for two or more children. The credit is available only to single parents or married couples where both parents work and is limited to the smaller earned income. It is not indexed.

Alternative Minimum Tax

The alternative minimum tax calculates a tax on a broader income base with a large flat exemption (in 2005, $58,000 for married couples and $40,250 for singles) and at rates of 26% and 28%. If this tax is higher than the regular tax, the difference in tax is added to the taxpayer's liability.

Currently the AMT does not affect very many taxpayers, but its effects will grow over time unless legislative changes are made, including a temporary increase in the exemption and indexing of the exemptions.

The alternative minimum tax originated in 1969 as an add-on tax on tax preferences and the most important preference was capital gains. At that time, there was an exclusion for a share of capital gains and the excluded share was taxed under the add-on tax. The add-on tax was eventually paired with and then displaced by the alternative minimum tax. In 1986 the capital gains preference was ended and the number of individuals affected by the tax, already small, fell further. Over time, however, the coverage of the AMT began to grow as rates increased and because the exemption was not indexed, while exemptions in the regular tax were. The potential coverage was also increased with the 2001 tax cut which cut regular rates but not AMT rates. The focus of preferences has also changed. The preference for capital gains enacted in 1997 and extended in 2003, and for dividends enacted in 2003 was not included in the AMT. Increasingly the major preference items are personal exemptions and certain itemized deductions. (The child credit was allowed against the AMT after it became clear that failure to do so would push many families onto the tax.) In the middle income classes, large families will increasingly be affected by the AMT, absent change.[9]

Other Provisions

In addition to these basic provisions — rate structures, personal exemptions, standard allowances, and credits — several other provisions related to family structure are summarized here. First, there are specific provisions that relate to family structure or characteristics. There are additional standard deductions for elderly and blind taxpayers (provisions that give little benefit to high income individuals who tend to itemize deductions). In addition, there is a 15% tax credit for the elderly and disabled that is phased out; since the base for the credit is offset by social security, it tends to benefit elderly and disabled individuals who do not receive social security. Another explicit family tax provision, adopted in 1986, is the "kiddie tax" which taxes unearned income of children under 14 at the parents' tax rate.

One might add a variety of exclusions (some social security benefits, welfare payments, in-kind benefits, employer provided child care) and deductions or credits (medical expenses, educational expenses) which benefit families of certain income levels and characteristics. Moreover, since the tax law does not apply to certain imputed income, families who prefer owner-occupied homes or in-home provision of goods and services, or the consumption of leisure over other goods, have greater tax benefits. These benefits are, in some cases, associated with family characteristics. For example, families with higher incomes and at certain ages are more likely to live in owner-occupied homes. One-earner married couples benefit from the services provided in the home by the non-working spouse which are not subject to tax.[10]

Finally, the payroll tax can alter the relative net tax burden between different types of families with consequences that could matter for concerns of equity and efficiency (such as work choice). The social security system may confer a marriage bonus, that can increase the implicit tax on work effort for second earners. Spouses receive a benefit, without necessarily paying any payroll taxes of their own; a second-earner spouse pays additional social security taxes but his or her benefit is only the net of a benefit based on the individual earnings record and the benefit for spouses — and this amount may not be positive. That is, the spouse's benefit based on the partner's earning record may be better than the benefit a spouse receives on his or her own earnings record, and there is, therefore, no return to payroll taxes paid. Thus, the net tax on a second earner spouse is effectively larger than it would be in the absence of a benefit for spouses, since little or no additional benefits occur as a result of those payments. There are also implicit taxes that affect behavior in the transfer system, where increases in income through work or marriage may cause a reduction in benefits, thereby discouraging these behaviors.

EQUITY AND DISTRIBUTIONAL ISSUES

Tax proposals can be evaluated on many grounds, but one issue is that of fairness. This issue of fairness can involve two elements: vertical equity, or the equity of changes in tax burdens as income rises for an otherwise identical family, and horizontal equity, or how taxes should be fairly differentiated between families of different sizes and structures. This analysis focuses primarily on the issue of horizontal equity, since this is an issue which can be addressed in a more analytical framework. We first, however, briefly discuss the issue of vertical equity.

Vertical Equity

The individual income tax is progressive in rate structure and in actual outcomes: higher income taxpayers pay larger shares of their income than do lower income taxpayers, and at the lowest income levels taxpayers received overall subsidies through the EIC. Because the desired degree of redistribution cannot be easily established, issues of vertical equity involve value judgments to a considerable degree.[11] By and large, the overall distribution of the tax system has not changed a great deal in the last twenty-three years; all tax rates have fallen and the largest reduction is for the very highest 1% of taxpayers, followed by the middle quintile. At the lower end, the earned income tax credits have more than offset growth in payroll taxes.[12]

How different tax revisions affect the progressivity of the income tax depends on several factors.

First, a significant fraction of taxpayers do not have income tax liability. Positive income taxes do not apply in most cases until individuals are above the poverty line. In the Tax Reform Act of 1986, the combination of standard deductions and personal exemptions were set to roughly approximate the poverty line — the income levels above which families of different sizes are not considered poor. The allowances for single individuals are below the poverty line and cause some poor single individuals to be taxed. The addition of the child credit means that taxpayers with qualifying children well above the poverty line would not be subject to tax. These taxpayers would not be affected by a tax cut.

An exception is when tax cuts are refundable. An expansion of the EIC, which is a refundable credit (or negative tax), would affect low-income individuals. The child credit is also refundable in some circumstances.

Certain types of revisions tend to benefit higher income individuals, while others tend to provide little benefit to that group. For example, while lowering the top rates clearly benefitted higher income individuals in 2001, it is also clear that widening the 15% rate bracket for joint returns also benefitted higher income individuals. In 2000, prior to the tax cut, according to the Internal Revenue Service's statistical data, of 129 million returns, approximately 69 million returns paid tax at the 15% rate and another 25 million had no tax liability. Thus the widening of the 15% bracket, which helped only those paying tax above that rate, benefitted approximately the top 25% of taxpayers. Higher income individuals are also more likely to itemize deductions, and changes which increase the standard deduction will tend to focus more benefits to moderate income taxpayers than high income ones. Similarly, expansions of benefits that are phased out, such as the child credits, would not benefit high income individuals. The 10% bracket also favored lower income families.

Horizontal Equity

Horizontal equity has to do with equal treatment of equals and is an important focus of this analysis. For the income tax, this standard might mean that families of the same size with the same income should pay the same tax. But, it could also be taken to mean that two individuals with the same income should pay the same tax. In a progressive tax system, these two standards can be incompatible, and, indeed this incompatibility causes marriage penalties and bonuses in a system where the family is the tax unit. Thus, the basic challenge of assessing standards of horizontal equity is to determine how to treat different taxpayers equitably. First, we review the economic principles which could be used in that assessment. Second, we consider in further detail the ability-to-pay concept, which seems most consistent with the equal-sacrifice principles of horizontal equity.

As the recent history of the tax law suggests and the following discussion reveals, tax policy has not generally been guided by a consistent theory of fairness or equity across different types of families. Indeed, it is clear that many of the structural changes in the treatment of the family were haphazard. Income splitting, perhaps one of the most important aspects of family tax differentials, was adopted in reaction to a legal situation. Other changes were contemporary reactions to a set of complaints or concerns about behavioral response (such as the singles rate schedule or attempts to fix the marriage penalty).

Theories of Equitable Taxation

For taxation purposes, there are two fundamental attributes of families: the type of head (a married couple, or a single individual) and the size. Families can be composed of single persons, single parents with children, childless couples, and married couples with children. And, in turn, there are two important features of the tax system that relate to these differences. First, should the unit of taxation be the individual, or the family? The U.S. tax system imposes taxes on families and differentiates in its rate structure between singles, head of households (single parents with children), and married couples. However, an alternative would be to apply a single rate schedule to each individual on his or her own earnings. While some preference for this view of individual taxation may have to do with philosophical matters, one argument for treating the individual rather than the family as a taxpaying unit has to do with marriage neutrality and efficiency, discussed subsequently. That is, if individuals could be taxed solely on their own earnings, there would be no tax consequences of being married, and the married state would not affect incentives to work via tax differentials.

The second issue is how one should adjust for family size, or, in the case of individual taxation, for the number of dependents. Despite the thrust of recent legislation that added substantial tax credits for children, some of the debate over differentiating by taxpayer characteristics has been over whether personal exemptions for dependents should be allowed at all. Under some theories of how the family should be taxed, no differentiation should be allowed for dependents; indeed, arguments are made that individuals should be taxed on their income without regard to their family arrangements. For that matter, individual taxation does not preclude allowances for number of dependents; rather, its focus is on treating working adults, even though married, as separate entities.[13] (In practice, such a tax system must always deal with the possibility of income splitting of capital income by transfers of assets within the family, as well as the allocation of deductions.)

Clearly the family involves a social and economic unit which differs from unrelated groupings. Although taxation of the family has received limited attention in the economics literature, various principles have been advanced about how to treat family characteristics. Three such approaches are outlined here: treating living arrangements and children as personal choices that should not be addressed by the tax law, equating post-tax standards of living for families with the same pretax standard of living, and family assistance.

This analysis does not consider another alternative principle of taxation, the benefit principle, which would set taxes to reflect the amount of government services received. One could argue that large families, particularly families with children, are greater beneficiaries of public spending, such as education. While some taxes are explicitly formulated as benefit taxes (e.g., the gasoline tax which is used to build roads), the individual income tax has generally been based on other principles, such as the ones described here.

Family Arrangements as Personal Choices

People are relatively free to choose whether to marry and have children, and an argument can be made that such choices should not lead to tax relief. From this perspective, if they choose to have children, they are not worse off, since the enjoyment they receive from their children outweighs any cost. Thus, one could think of children as part of the consumption of the parents.[14] At a minimum, this approach suggests that no allowance be made for the additional cost of supporting children, treating the choice to have children as a consumption item, no different from the decision to consume food or clothing. Similarly, the choice of a spouse could be seen as a consumption or investment choice, which should not alter the tax paid by the individual, or the combined tax of the two spouses. In this case, the individual should be the tax unit.

While the argument that children constitute consumption to their parents may be a defensible one, using this view as a guide to making tax policy is problematic. Even if the adults have made a choice, a troublesome aspect of this treatment of children as consumption is that it considers only the well-being of the parent or parents. Parents' tastes for children aside, the material level of consumption for children as well as for adults is affected by the number of others in the family.

Some theories have suggested that children could be seen as an investment, perhaps for support in old age. There is some justification for this theory of parental motivation, although it must surely be less than universal since many parents leave bequests to their children, rather than being supported by them in old age. If investment were the objective of having children, then there would be some justification for tax relief, since the cost of such an investment should, in theory, be recovered; at the same time, returns (such as help in old age) should be taxed to the parents. Our tax system is not designed along these lines, and, in any case, the children-as-investment theory also suffers from a lack of focus on the well-being of the children.

Ability to Pay Approaches

Another approach is simply that of ability to pay, which is the cornerstone of progressive taxation. Applying this ability-to-pay standard of taxation is straightforward in theory if one begins with the proposition that families with equal standards of living before tax should have equal standards of living after tax. If all family members were more or less identical in their needs and if all goods consumed were purely private in nature, this standard would suggest full income splitting of total family income among all members of the family. One could merely divide all family income evenly and then subject each share to an identical rate structure. In a progressive tax system, larger families would pay smaller taxes than smaller families with the same total income.

One difficulty with this straightforward prescription is the existence of "club" goods within the family. Some goods are more or less purely private goods, such as food. If one person consumes food, it is not available to anyone else. Other goods have elements of a club nature (one person can consume the good without interfering with another's consumption). Such club goods include housing and some furnishings, reading materials, and the family car. None of these goods are pure shared goods since tastes may not be identical and congestion may occur, but they do provide scale advantages in consumption within a family. These scale advantages in family consumption are recognized in construction of the poverty line, which varies with family size, yet does not increase in full proportion to it.

Another problem is that adults and children may differ in the amount of private goods they need or desire.

If we knew how to scale ability to pay by family size and characteristics, design of the income tax would be theoretically straightforward. The method would be as follows. Choose a representative family (e.g., a family of two). Devise the tax rate schedule to achieve the desired degree of progression, setting the exempt level at the poverty level or whatever other level is desired. The solution to horizontal equity is then, simply, an averaging approach. For example, consider a larger family which needs 50% more income than the basic reference family. This means that a larger family that has $75,000 of income should have the same average tax rate as a smaller (reference) family with $50,000 of income. We simply apply the basic tax rate schedule to two thirds of the larger family's income, and multiply the resulting tax liability by 1.5. This approach will produce the same effective tax rate for the larger family as for the reference family. (The larger family, which has more income, will still pay more taxes, but the fraction paid will be the same as the smaller family.) The two families will have the same (although smaller) standard of living after tax just as they had the same standard of living before tax.

When exempt levels of tax are set roughly at the poverty rate, as was the intent of the 1986 Tax Reform Act, families whose income falls within the first rate bracket (the 15% tax bracket at that point) tend to have equal effective tax rates, if the relative poverty measures across families are correct (ignoring the earned income tax credit). These effects will not hold, however, when higher income families are considered or when other provisions, such as the child credit and the earned income credit, are considered, or with a new small bracket such as the 10% bracket introduced in 2001. Moreover, families with one earner are better off than families with two earners at the same income because of the expenses of working, including child care, and the benefits of home production of the non-working spouse. Thus, credits for child care expenses or allowances for working spouses can move the system towards more equitable treatment, at least vis-a-vis one-earner couples.

Targeted Family Assistance

At the opposite end of the spectrum is the notion of targeted family assistance, especially for lower income families, and often targeted towards children. To accomplish this targeting, allowances for family size differentials (e.g., personal allowances) are often made refundable, they take the form of a credit rather than an exemption, and benefits are often phased out as incomes rise. Several of these features, including the EIC and the child credit, have made their way into current law.

This view of family allowances differs from the philosophy that personal exemptions, along with other exclusions, should be used to exempt a minimum subsistence amount from the income base, the philosophy underlying the 1986 revisions, and one which is more in line with the ability to pay standard. Similarly, a benefit for child care would be more appropriately made through a deduction, if child care was viewed as one of the costs of working under an ability-to-pay approach.

Proposals that are driven by this philosophy are often simultaneously addressing differentiation across family types and a vertical distribution objective. This objective is not necessarily inconsistent with the ability-to-pay objective addressed previously, even though it often appears to be because of the mechanisms chosen, such as credits that are phased out. For a given family size, any degree of vertical equity can be obtained through either exemptions or credits or by arranging the tax rate schedule appropriately. But, the differentiation across families at the same income level (or ability-to-pay) can be achieved only by selecting the sizes of personal exemptions for different family members. An ability-to-pay approach would include differentiation of families of different sizes at either high or low income levels. When a vanishing exemption or credit is chosen in the interest of vertical equity, the actual result is to allow no differentiation for family size at higher income levels.[15]

Finally, it is important to recognize that the income tax system exists side by side with a welfare system and many conclude that targeted family assistance might better be addressed through the welfare system.

APPLYING THE ABILITY-TO-PAY HORIZONTAL EQUITY STANDARD TO CURRENT LAW

The ability to pay approach seems the most consistent and, to many, appealing of the three approaches to dealing with tax differentiation based on family size. This method considers the welfare of all in society rather than focusing exclusively on adults or children. A recent study used this approach to estimate effective tax rates in 2005, and how various provisions of the tax law affected these rates, using an equivalency scale similar to the variations in poverty lines across family types.[16]

The remainder of this section reports the results of that study. In defining families that have the same ability to pay, an adjustment based on a research study similar to that adjusting for official poverty levels for different family sizes was used which has a smaller adjustment for children than for adults. Under this standard, a single person requires about 62% of the income of a married couple; a couple with four kids requires about three times the income. Thus, for a married couple with no children with $20,000 of income, an equivalent single person would need slightly over $12,000 and a married couple with four children would need $60,000.

Table 1 reports the 2005 effective tax rates for low- and middle-income taxpayers at different levels of income, for family sizes of up to seven individuals, and for the three basic types of returns — single, joint, and head of household, without considering the child credit. Table 2 reports the tax rates for higher income families. the heading of the column indicates the income level for married couples. Families in each column have the same estimated ability to pay, so that larger families have more income and singles and a head of household with one child have less. The rates across families should be compared by looking down the columns. For example, in table 1, a married couple with $25,000 in income pays 3.4% of income in taxes, but a married couple with one child with the same ability to pay receives a subsidy of 0.7%, while a single with an equivalent before tax standard of living pays 4.7%.

These numbers assume that dependents are children eligible for the child credit and that the families are eligible for the earned income tax credit (a provision not allowed for those over 65 or for those without children under 25). These are illustrative calculations that do not account for any other tax preferences and are designed to show how the basic structural, family-related features of the tax law affect burdens. Tax rates for returns paying the AMT are bolded.

These tables suggest that the pattern of tax burden by family size varies across the income scale, as it reflects the complications of the earned income tax credit, the child credit, and graduated rates, including phase-out effects. Moreover, the variation across families which have the same ability to pay is substantial. At low incomes, families with children, whether headed by a married couple or a single parent, are favored because of the earned income tax credit. The largest negative tax rates tend to accrue to returns with two children, since the largest EIC credits are available for these returns.

Table 1. Average Effective Income Tax Rates by Type of Return, Family Size, and Income: Lower and Middle Incomes (2005 tax law and income levels)

	Income Level for Married Couple			
Type-Size	$10,000	$15,000	$25,000	$50,000
Single - 1	-6.5%	-1.0%	4.7%	9.0%
Joint - 2	-2.9	0.0	3.4	8.3
Joint - 3	-23.2	-17.9	-0.7	6.6
Joint - 4	-34.0	-22.4	-2.4	5.3
Joint - 5	-31.4	-18.9	-3.5	4.3
Joint - 6	-27.5	-16.3	-4.8	3.5
Joint - 7	-24.5	-14.3	-6.2	3.0
H/H - 2	-29.8	-22.6	-6.8	6.4
H/H - 3	-39.2	-27.6	-7.9	4.7
H/H - 4	-35.2	-22..7	-5.2	3.7
H/H - 5	-30.8	-18.5	-6.0	4.9
H/H - 6	-26.7	-15.8	-7.4	6.3
H/H - 7	-23.5	-13.7	-8.6	7.4

Source: Gravelle and Gravelle. The dollar amounts refer to the income for a married couple with no children; larger families in each column would have more income and singles and heads of household with 2 family members (one child) would have less income.

Table 2. Average Effective Income Tax Rates by Type of Return, Family Size, and Income: Higher Incomes (2005 tax law and income levels)

	Income Level for a Married Couple of Two			
Type-Size	$75,000	$100,000	$250,000	$500,000
Single - 1	10.5%	12.8%	17.8%	24.2%
Joint - 2	9.5	11.2	19.4	24.8
Joint - 3	8.6	11.9	21.8	24.9
Joint - 4	8.6	12.5	23.4	25.0
Joint - 5	9.0	14.0	24.4	25.1
Joint - 6	10.3	15.5	24.7	25.4
Joint - 7	11.4	16.7	24.8	25.6
H/H - 2	8.9	12.4	21.3	24.6
H/H - 3	9.7	13.6	23.6	24.9
H/H - 4	11.2	15.7	24.3	25.0
H/H - 5	12.6	17.6	24.5	25.3
H/H - 6	13.8	18.9	24.6	25.6
H/H - 7	15.1	19.9	24.7	25.9

Source: Gravelle and Gravelle. The dollar amounts refer to the income for a married couple with no children; larger families in each column would have more income and singles and heads of household with 2 family members (one child) would have less income.

As incomes rise, families with children are still favored, but it is the largest families that have the largest subsidies or the smallest tax rates, because of the combination of the personal exemptions and the child credit lower taxes so much for these families. Eventually large families began to be penalized because the value of the child credit and personal exemptions relative to income declines and larger families that require more income are pushed up through the rate brackets. That effect is increased because more families with children are subjected to the AMT. At higher income levels, credits and exemptions begin to be phased out. As incomes reach very high levels, however, the rates converge as the tax becomes large a flat tax. (Note that itemized deductions assumed to be a constant fraction of income, and so is a proportional exclusion).

Overall, these calculations suggest (1) that singles are taxed more heavily than childless couples in the middle income ranges but less heavily at very high and very low income levels; (2) when the child credit and EIC are available, families with children tend to be favored over families without children at low and moderate income levels; (3) the number of children in a family sometimes causes more beneficial treatment and sometimes less depending on how the EIC and child credit are being phased out; and (4) the graduated rate structure causes large families at higher income levels to be taxed significantly more, an effect exacerbated by the AMT.

These results can be characterized as resulting from the fundamental structural flaws of phase-out provisions and rate brackets. Phase-out points and rate brackets should be based on family size if the ability to pay criterion is being used to determine the tax structure. The flat amount of the child credit and personal exemption also causes them to have little effect on relative tax liabilities at high income levels; phasing them out increases the over-taxation of large families relative to small ones at higher income levels

At low income levels, however, the family comparisons are affected by the earned-income tax credit, and differences in tax burdens by family size can be striking. If there were no earned-income tax credit, effective tax rates would be relatively uniform at the lower income levels, at zero or a small positive percentage amount. The EIC introduces disparities. First, the EIC rate is much lower for single taxpayers or two-member joint returns where there are no qualifying children than it is for families with children. Second, if one accepts the ability-to-pay standard, the EIC has an inappropriate adjustment for family size. There is no reason to vary the rate of the EIC by family size; but the base (or maximum creditable wage) and the phase-out levels should be varied according to the ability-to-pay standard. That is, both dollar amounts — the amount on which the EIC applies and the income at which the phase-out begins — should be tied to family size according to the ability to pay standard, while the EIC rate should be the same for all families.

To make the EIC neutral across families, using the ability-to-pay standard, would require, in addition to allowing it at a common rate for all families, changing the base levels and the phase-out levels for family size. Changing the rate, as was done in 1990 and retained when the EIC was expanded in 1993, does not accomplish equal treatment across families of different sizes, providing too much adjustment for some families and not enough for others.

The analysis also considered the effects of other aspects of the tax system. One is the availability of the child care credit. The analysis in that paper indicated that including the child credit (at the maximum) does not have very important effects. The dependent care credit is not effectively available to low income families who do not have sufficient tax liability to use the credit, and is capped and unimportant in a relative sense for high income taxpayers. In the middle income levels, it lowers the tax rate for families with children.

Another issue has to do with the treatment of married couples where only one individual works outside the home. These families are better off because the spouse not employed outside the home can perform services at home which result in cost savings, perform household tasks which increase leisure time for the rest of the family, or enjoy leisure. The value of this time, which is not counted in the measured transactions of the economy, is referred to as "imputed income." This imputed income is not taxed, and it would probably be impractical to tax it. Nevertheless, the tax burden as a percent of cash plus imputed income is lower for such a family.

Imputed income is not easily valued and this issue is explored in the study by limiting the imputed income to the value of child care using the cap for the expenses eligible for a child care credit and excluding this amount from income. For low income families, this change actually increased taxes by reducing earned income credits. At moderate and middle incomes, it benefitted married couples with children, who already tend to be favored.

The authors also considered some of the potential changes and whether those would increase horizontal equity or exacerbate it. In the interest of increased horizontal equity, the analysis would support an increase in the earned income credit for those without children; a reduction (or containment) of the AMT which will grow in importance absent change; and elimination of phase-outs for child credits, personal exemptions, and itemized deductions. (2001 tax law changes proposed to eliminate the phase-out of the latter two beginning in 2007.) Making the child credit fully refundable would increase disparities in tax rates at the lower income levels.

These calculations should be considered with caution, as they depend on the precision of the family equivalency scales, which do not take into account the heterogeneity of the cost of rearing children, and are aimed at measuring cash needs to attain a given standard of living. Lower income families with younger children who need child care may find their standard of living in material matters lower than other types of families, because of the higher cost of that care relative to their income. In that case, the lower rates due to child care credits or exclusion of imputed income may be appropriate. At higher income levels, child care costs are probably much smaller relative to income, even if more is spent on care. The child care credit, however, has little effect on effective tax rates at these income levels.

Marriage Penalties and Marriage Bonuses

Concerns about the marriage penalty reflect a reluctance to penalize marriage in a society that upholds such traditions. As the tax law shifts to reduce the marriage penalty, as it did in 2001, it also expands marriage bonuses. These choices have consequences not only for incentives but for equitable treatment of singles and married couples. As shown above in tables 1 and 2, in the middle income brackets, where the marriage penalty was largely eliminated, singles with the same ability to pay are subject to higher taxes than married couples. Singles benefit at lower income levels because their lower required incomes do not phase them out of the earned income credit. And at very high incomes married couples may pay a larger share of their income because of marriage penalties that remain in the AMT and the upper brackets of the rate structure.

This section explores the treatment of married couples and singles in an additional dimension by assuming that singles live together and share the same economies of scale that married couples do. These individuals could be room mates, but they could also be partners who differ from married couples only in that they are not legally married.[17] Single individuals who live together in the same fashion as married couples have the same ability to pay with the same income. However, remaining single can alter their tax liability. Remaining single can cause tax liability either to rise or fall, depending on the split of income between the two spouses. If one individual earns most of the income, tax burdens will be higher for two individuals who are not married than for a married couple with the same total income, because the standard deductions are smaller and the rate brackets narrower. If income is evenly split between the two individuals, there can be a benefit from remaining single. Married individuals have to combine their income, and the rate brackets for joint returns at the higher income brackets, while wider than those for single individuals, are not twice as wide. At all levels they are not wider than those for heads of household.

The marriage penalty or bonus might, in the context of the measures of household ability-to-pay, also be described as a singles bonus or penalty. In any case, in considering both the incentive and equity dimension to this issue, the tax rates of these families should be compared to the tax rates of other households.

Tables 3 and 4 show the effective tax rates for married couples and for unmarried couples with the same combined income, both where income is evenly split and where all income is received by one person. In one case there is no child and in the other a single child. These income splits represent the extremes of the marriage penalty and the marriage bonus. The same reference income classes and equivalency scales in tables 1 and 2 are used.

Note that uneven income splits in the case of a family with a child can yield different results depending on whether the individual with the income can claim the child and therefore receive the benefits of the head of household rate structure, the higher earned income credit, the dependency exemption, and the child credit. If not, that individual files as a single.

The tables indicate that both marriage penalties and bonuses persist. In the case of families without children, however, penalties do not exist in the middle income ranges, only bonuses. In this case, singles who live together and who have uneven incomes would see their tax rates fall if they got married. Both bonuses and penalties exist at the lower income levels because of the earned income tax credit. If income is evenly split, the phase out ranges are not reached as quickly for singles because each of the partners has only half the income. If all of the income is earned by one of the singles in the single partnership, phase out of the credit still occurs and the individual also has a smaller standard deduction, and thus pays a higher tax. The smaller deductions and narrower rate brackets also cause the higher tax rates through the middle income brackets. At very high income levels, marriage penalties can also occur. Some of the penalty is due to not doubling the rate brackets after the 15% bracket, but more of it is due to the marriage penalties in the AMT. If there were no AMT, tax rates for joint returns would be 17.1% and 22.8% for the $250,000 and $500,000 incomes. The regular tax is still responsible for most of the penalty for singles with one partner earning income: the regular rates are 20.9% and 24.1% for the $250,000 and $500,000 incomes.

Matters are more complex for families with one child. At low income levels, and a 50/50 split, one of the singles files a single return with a very limited negative rate because of the small earned income credit for those without children, while the other claims a child and has a much higher negative tax rate than a married couple because there is no phase out of benefits. The result is that there is a marriage bonus. This eventually becomes a marriage penalty because of the favorable head of household standard deduction and rate structure. The penalty continues through all the incomes shown, although it eventually becomes very small at the top. A small part of this penalty is due to the AMT at the $250,000 equivalent incomes: the rates without the AMT for a joint return is 19.7% and the rate for the combined singles 16.8%. Eliminating the AMT would, however, widen the discrepancy between the two at the

$500,000 equivalent level: without the AMT the rates would be 23.9% for a joint return and 21.6% for the combined singles.

Table 3. Average Effective Income Tax Rates for Joint Returns and Unmarried Couples, By Size of Income and Degree of Split: Lower and Middle Incomes (2005 Levels of Income)

	Income Level for Married Couple			
Type-Size	$10,000	$15,000	$25,000	$50,000
No Child				
Joint	-2.9	0.0	3.4	8.3
Single 50/50 Split	- 7.7	- 4.3	3.4	6.6
Single 100/0 Split	0.5	4.5	8.3	11.2
One Child				
Joint	-23.2	-17.9	-0.7	6.6
50/50 Split (One	-19.9	-15.0	-7.9	6.1
Single, One Head of				
Household				
100/0 Split, Single	3.5	6.4	9.0	12.8
Return				
100/0 Split, Head of	-23.2	-13.6	3.3	8.0
Household Return				

Source: Congressional Research Service. Note that effective tax rate does not always rise across incomes due to rounding.

Table 4. Average Effective Income Tax Rates for Joint Returns and Unmarried Couples, By Size of Income and Degree of Split: Higher Incomes (2005 Levels of Income)

	Income Level for Married Couple			
Type	$75,000	$100,000	$250,000	$500,000
No Child				
Joint	9.5 %	11.2 %	19.4 %	24.8 %
Single 50/50 Split	9.5	11.2	16.7	22.4
Single 100/0 Split	14.0	15.5	22.4	24.8
One Child				
Joint	8.6	11.9	21.8	24.9
50/50 Split (One Single, One Head of Household)	8.5	10.4	17.6	24.2
100/0 Split, Single Return	15.0	16.6	24.2	25.0
100/0 Split, Head of Household Return	12.1	14.6	24.2	25.0

Source: Congressional Research Service. Note that effective tax rate does not always rise across incomes due to rounding.

With one of the pair earning all of the income, the results depend on whether the partner with the income can claim the child. If that person cannot, the tax burden is higher throughout the scale (although it reaches roughly the same level at the highest level in part because of the AMT). The discrepancy at the $250,000 level is increased slightly by the AMT (the regular rates are 19.7% for the joint return and 22.1% for the single). If the person with the income can claim the child, joint returns are still favored, but not by nearly as much.

Which of these last two assumptions seems more likely depends on the circumstances. When couples divorce, they typically move to different residences and the most usual outcome is that the mother who typically has lower earnings would have the child. According to the Census Bureau, 83% of children who live with one parent live with their mother.[18] In that case, the comparisons in tables 1 and 2 would be appropriate. If the couple divorce but live together, presumably the higher income spouse would claim the child. However, if a couple never married and the child is only related to one parent, that person, more likely the mother and more likely to have low income, would claim the child. If such a couple married and had low incomes, they could obtain the earned income credit and a study of low income families indicates that this latter effect, the bonus, is the most common effect of the EIC.[19]

Which circumstances are more characteristic of the economy? Note first that, although people refer to the marriage penalty for a particular family situation or the aggregate size of the marriage penalty, it is really not possible, in many cases, to determine the size of the penalty or bonus. The effect of assignment of a child is demonstrated in tables 3 and 4, but other features matter. Only when a married couple has only earned income, no dependent children, and no itemized deductions or other special characteristics, and only if it is assumed that their behavior would not have been different if their marital status had been different, can one actually measure the size of the marriage penalty or bonus. There is no way to know who would have custody of the children and therefore which of the partners might be eligible for head of household status and for the accompanying personal exemptions and child credits.

There is reason to expect that unmarried individuals are penalized in the aggregate. Prior to the 2001 tax cut, which increased bonuses and reduced penalties, using an allocation that reflects typical behavior of married couples with respect to child custody, the Congressional Budget Office (CBO) estimated that 37% of married couples had penalties ($24 billion), 3% were unaffected, and 60% had bonuses ($73 billion). (Itemized deductions and earned income were assigned in proportion to earnings). The net bonus was $49 billion.[20] However, in most of its analysis, the CBO study relied on a measure of marriage penalties and bonuses that assumed child custody would be based on a tax-minimizing strategy. For example, if parents of two children had similar individual earnings, each would be assumed to have custody of one of the children so that both would be eligible for head-of-household status. Even using that standard, net bonuses occurred: 43% of married couples had penalties amounting to $32 billion, and 52% had bonuses of $43 billion, for a net bonuses of $11 billion. Nevertheless, a significant proportion of married taxpayers — between 37% and 43% — paid marriage penalties.

A study using Treasury data and other assumptions produced different measures of the marriage bonus or penalty.[21] Using an assumption that divorced parents occupied the same residence, and thus only one could qualify for head of household status, the authors found that 48% had a penalty ($28.3 billion) and 41% had a bonus ($26.7 billion), for a net penalty of $1.6 billion. This study also provided several other ways of measuring penalties and bonuses, including estimating $30.2 billion in singles penalties because these individuals could not use joint return rate schedules. Some of the penalty applied to families with children because of the benefits of head of household status. Without head-of-household status, the Treasury found that 46% of couples have bonuses ($36.6 billion), 43% had penalties ($20.8 billion) and the net effect was a bonus of $15.8 billion.

Treasury researchers did a subsequent study using the standard assumption for the effects of the 2001 tax cut and for 2004 income levels.[22] As before, they essentially found a penalty (of $3.7 billion) without the 2001 tax cut, but found a $30 billion bonus with 2004 tax law (which included explicit marriage relief provisions and other provisions such as rate reductions). About 60% of couples have bonuses, and 23% have penalties (while some have no effect). The study also warns that penalties will grow substantially if the AMT continues to grow as projected.

Given the shift away from penalties and towards bonuses in 2001, it seems clear that the current situation is characterized by bonuses rather than penalties. However, if the AMT is allowed to grow and begins to cover many taxpayers, more significant penalties will return.

An alternative measurement is the bonuses and penalties of single individuals who are cohabitating, a much smaller group of people. In 2005, according to the Census Bureau, there were 58 million married households, but only 5 million unmarried couple households (with partners of the opposite sex).[23] (There were 77 million households altogether). Thus, assuming that these households were similar to married households, the "single penalties and bonuses" measured by looking at unmarried cohabitating households would be about 9% of the size of "marriage bonuses and penalties" measured by looking at married households.

A study has been made of penalties and bonuses for existing co-habiting couples with children, which assign the children to the biological parent, or, if both partners are biological parents to the higher earner.[24] This study found that under 2003 law, 42% of these couples would experience a bonus averaging $1,893 while 50.7% would experience a penalty of $1,497. Under 2003 law, 48.5% receive an average bonus of $2,236 and 44.1% receive a penalty of $1,513. Bonuses are actually more prevalent in low income households because marriage often increases the earned income credit.

In general, therefore, the rules tend to indicate that singles who are living together are, on average, being penalized relative to married couples, but this pattern does not hold for all circumstances.

The marriage penalty cannot be easily addressed because we cannot simultaneously achieve three apparently desired income tax objectives: a progressive tax, a marriage neutral tax, and equal treatment of couples with the same total incomes, but with different income shares. Moreover, even if one were to chose horizontal equity, the achievement of that system would require information on living arrangements of unmarried individuals that is not available to the tax authorities. The current system, however, appears to lean towards benefitting marriage, as long as the AMT is contained.

SUMMARY

The analysis of equity across families suggests that, based on an ability to pay standard, families with children are paying lower rates of tax (or receiving larger negative tax rates) than single individuals and married couples at lower and middle incomes, while families with children are being taxed more heavily at higher income levels. At the lowest income levels, the EIC provides the largest tax subsidies to single parents with two children, followed by single parents with three children and married couples with two children. The smallest subsidies go to childless couples, but all families with children have much larger subsidies than either childless couples or single individuals. At middle income levels, families with many children will have the most favorable treatment, due to the effect of the child credit which has a very large effect relative to tax liability. At higher income levels, large families are penalized because the adjustments for children such as personal exemptions and child credits are too small or are phased out, while graduated rates cause larger families that need more income to maintain a given living standard to pay higher taxes. Tax rates are more variable at lower income levels. At all but the lowest and very highest income levels, singles pay higher taxes than married couples.

After the 2001 tax cut, the vast majority of taxpayers without children receive a marriage bonus rather than a penalty, with penalties occurring only at the bottom and at the top — the latter due largely to the AMT. The comparison of families with children is less easily defined. Overall, marriage appears to be rewarded, but if the AMT continues to increase its scope (as it will absent legislation) penalties will begin to reach back in the middle income classes.

REFERENCES

[1] The ratio of prices in 2005 to those in 1948 using the GDP deflator is 7.03, while personal exemptions have increased from $600 to $3200, a ratio of 5.33.

[2] In general, floors and ceilings for standard deductions for joint returns were halved for married couples filing separate returns.

[3] In 2005, the personal exemption was $3,200 and the standard deduction $10,000, for a total of $22,800. The exempt allowance in 1948 was $2,667 (600 times 4 divided by 0.9). If the 1948 levels had kept pace with the GDP deflator, the total amount would be $20,177.

[4] Kyle Mudry and Michael Parisi, Individual Income Tax Rates and Shares, Internal Revenue Service *Statistics of Income Bulletin*, 2003, posted at [http://www.irs.ustreas.gov/taxstats/indtaxstats/article/0,,id=129270,00.html#_article]

[5] Details of the tax rates can be found in CRS Report RL30007, *Individual Income Tax Rates 1989-2007*, by Gregg Esenwein.

[6] The itemized deduction phase-out range, which is indexed for inflation, begins at $145,950 for 2005; the personal exemption phase-out, which is also indexed, varies by type of return, but begins at about $145,950 for singles. The top rate of 35% begins at $326,450 of *taxable* income. Child credits begin to phase out at about $75,000 for head of household returns and $110,000 for joint returns.

[7] Internal Revenue Service, *Statistics of Income*, posted at [http://www.irs.ustreas.gov/taxstats/indtaxstats/article/0,,id=96981,00.html#_grp1].

[8] Although there were two statutory rate brackets after 1986, 15% and 28%, there was also a surcharge that was designed to phase out the benefits of the 15% rate and the personal exemptions for high income taxpayers. This surcharge effectively increased the tax rate by 5 percentage points, to 33%, and created a bubble: rates were 15%, then 28%, then 33%, and then fell back to 28%.

[9] For a more detailed discussion and history, see CRS Report RL30149, *The Alternative Minimum Tax for Individuals*, by Gregg Esenwein.

[10] This concept be may unfamiliar, particularly to readers who think of spouses working at home as making a monetary sacrifice, perhaps to stay with their children. While their income is smaller, they save the taxes that would have been paid on outside earnings. However, these spouses do not give up all of their income, since there are cost savings, as in lower child care payments or not having to pay for other services (e.g., dry

cleaning, household help). It is this value that provides a benefit to one-earner families and is the imputed income not subject to tax.

[11] Progressivity in the tax system is typically based on an equal sacrifice notion and the notion that a dollar to a poor person is much more valuable than a dollar to the wealthy person. These theories do not easily pin down the desired degree of progressivity, however. For a more extensive discussion of distributional issues and of the distribution of the income tax see CRS Report RL32693, *Distribution of the Tax Burden Across Individuals: An Overview*, by Jane G. Gravelle and Maxim Shvedov.

[12] See Congressional Budget Office, *Historical Effective Federal Tax Rates: 1979 to 2003*, December 2005: [http://www.cbo.gov/ftpdoc.cfm?index=7000 and type=1].

[13] See Harvey E. Brazer, "Income Tax Treatment of the Family;" and Alicia Munnell, "TheCouple vs. The Individual under the Federal Personal Income Tax;" both in *The Economics of Taxation*, ed. Henry J. Aaron and Michael J. Boskin, Washington, DC, Brookings Institution, 1980.

[14] The notion of children as consumption can be traced to Henry Simons, *Personal Income Taxation*, Chicago: University of Chicago Press, 1938.

[15] One argument along these lines is that progressive taxation could be justified by the need to maintain human resources at the bottom of the scale (which justifies some minimum exclusion) and curb the accumulation of power at the top. Since the accumulation of power is undiminished by family size, there should be little differentiation at the top of the scale. See Harold M. Groves, *Federal Tax Treatment of the Family*, Washington, DC, The Brookings Institution, 1963.

[16] Jane Gravelle and Jennifer Gravelle, "Horizontal Equity and Family Tax Treatment: The Orphan Child of Tax Policy," *National Tax Journal*, vol 59, Sept. 2006, pp. 631-649. This study calculated stylized effective tax rates reflecting personal exemptions, itemized or standard deductions, the child credit, and the earned income credit The equivalency formula used was $(A+0.7K)^{0.7}$ based on Constance F. Citro and Robert T. Michael, *Measuring Poverty: A New Approach*, Washington, DC, National Academy Press, 1995. Using this formula, a single person would need 62% of the income of a married couple without children to achieve the same standard of income. A married couple with one child would need 23% more and a married couple with two children would need 45% more.

[17] For other discussions of this issue see Gregg Esenwein, *The Individual Income Tax and Marriage Neutrality*, Congressional Research Service, Library of Congress, Report No. 88-8 E, December 21, 1987; Daniel Feenberg, "The Tax Treatment of Married Couples and the 1981 Tax Law," In *Taxing the Family*, Ed. Rudolph G. Penner, Washington: American Enterprise Institute for Public Policy Research, 1983; Harvey Rosen, "The Marriage Tax is Down But Not Out," *National Tax Journal*, Vol. 40, December, 1987, pp 567-576; Daniel R. Feenberg and Harvey S. Rosen." Recent Developments in the Marriage Tax." *National Tax Journal*, Vol. 48, March 1995, pp. 91-101. Rosen, Harvey, "Is It Time to Abandon Joint Filing?" *National Tax Journal*, Vol. 30 (December 1977): 423-428. U.S. Congressional Budget Office. *For Better or for Worse: Marriage and the Federal Income Tax*. Washington , DC, June 1997.

[18] U.S. Census Bureau, table C2: Household Relationships and Living Arrangements of Children Under 18: [http://www.census.gov/population/www/socdemo/hh-fam/cps2005.html]

[19] See Stacy Dickert-Conlin and Scott Houser. "Taxes and Transfers: A New Look at the Marriage Penalty." *National Tax Journal* 51, June 1998, pp. 175-217.

[20] These and other numbers discussed in this paragraph are from an update of a study by the U.S.. Congressional Budget Office, *For Better or for Worse: Marriage and the Federal Income Tax*. Washington , DC, June 1997. These numbers were updated for 1999 in a memorandum from Bob Williams and David Weiner of CBO dated September 18, 1998.

[21] Nicholas Bull, Janet Holtzblatt, James R. Nunns, and Robert Rebelein. Assessing Marriage Penalties and Bonuses. *Proceedings of the 91st Annual Conference of the National Tax Association*, 1998, pp. 327-340. An updated version of this paper is published as Office of Tax Analysis Paper 82, Defining and Measuring Marriage Penalties and Bonuses, November 1999 [http://www.ustreas.gov/ota/ota82_revised.pdf].

[22] Robert Gillette, Janet Holtzblatt, and Emily Y. Yin, Marriage Penalties and Bonuses: A Longer Term, Proceeding of the National Tax Association, 2004, Washington, DC, National Tax Association, pp. 468-478.

[23] [http://www.census.gov/population/www/socdemo/hh-fam/cps2005.html]

[24] Elaine Maag, "Taxes and Marriage for Cohabiting Parents," *Tax Notes,* May 23, 2005, p. 1031.

In: Families: Rights, Laws and Stability
Editors: J. R. Redmund, K. B. Killigan, pp. 53-74
ISBN: 978-1-60456-203-3

Chapter 3

FATHERHOOD INITIATIVES: CONNECTING FATHERS TO THEIR CHILDREN*

Carmen Solomon-Fears

ABSTRACT

In 2005, 23% of families with children were maintained by mothers. According to some estimates, 60% of children born during the 1990s will spend a significant portion of their childhood in a home without their father. Research indicates that children raised in single-parent families are more likely than children raised in two-parent families (with both biological parents) to do poorly in school, have emotional and behavioral problems, become teenage parents, and have poverty-level incomes. In hopes of improving the long-term outlook for children in single-parent families, federal, state, and local governments, along with public and private organizations, are supporting programs and activities that promote the financial and personal responsibility of noncustodial fathers to their children and increase the participation of fathers in the lives of their children. These programs have come to be known as "responsible fatherhood" programs.

Sources of federal funding for fatherhood programs include the Temporary Assistance for Needy Families (TANF) program, TANF state Maintenance-of-Effort (MOE) funding, welfare-to-work funds, Child Support Enforcement (CSE) funds, and Social Services Block Grant (Title XX) funds.

Beginning with the 106th Congress, the House but not the Senate passed bills containing specific funding for responsible fatherhood initiatives (in the 107th and 108th Congresses as part of welfare reauthorization bills). Moreover, from the start President Bush has been a supporter of responsible fatherhood programs; each of his budgets has included funding for such programs. In the 109th Congress, P.L. 109-171 — the Deficit Reduction Act of 2005 — was enacted. It included a provision that provides up to $50 million per year (FY2006-FY2010) in competitive grants to states, territories, Indian tribes and tribal organizations, and public and nonprofit community groups (including religious organizations) for responsible fatherhood initiatives.

* Excerpted from CRS Report RL31025, dated July 25, 2007.

Most fatherhood programs include media campaigns that emphasize the importance of emotional, physical, psychological, and financial connections of fathers to their children. Most fatherhood programs include parenting education; responsible decision-making; mediation services for both parents; providing an understanding of the CSE program; conflict resolution, coping with stress, and problem-solving skills; peer support; and job-training opportunities (skills development, interviewing skills, job search, job-retention skills, job-advancement skills, etc.). To help fathers and mothers meet their parental responsibilities, many policy analysts and observers support broad-based collaborative strategies that go beyond welfare and child support agencies and include schools, work programs, prison systems, churches, community organizations, and the health care system.

The federal government's support of fatherhood initiatives raises a wide array of issues. This article briefly examines the role of the CSE agency in fatherhood programs, discusses initiatives to promote and support father-child interaction outside the framework of the father-mother relationship, and summarizes the debate over whether fatherhood programs should include the "promotion of marriage."

INTRODUCTION

In 2005, 28% of families with children (under age 18) were maintained by one parent;[1] this figure is up from 11% in 1970. Most of the children in these single-parent families were being raised by their mothers; in 2005, 23% were in mother-only families and 5% in father-only families. According to some estimates, 60% of children born during the 1990s will spend a significant portion of their childhood in a home without their biological father. Research indicates that children raised in single-parent families are more likely than children raised in two-parent families (with both biological parents) to do poorly in school, have emotional and behavioral problems, become teenage parents, and have poverty-level incomes as adults.[2] Nonetheless, it is widely acknowledged that most of these mothers, despite the added stress of being a single parent, do a good job raising their children. That is, although children with absent fathers are at greater risk of having the aforementioned problems, most do not experience them. In hopes of improving the long-term outlook for children in single-parent families, federal, state, and local governments along with public and private organizations are supporting programs and activities that promote the financial and personal responsibility of noncustodial fathers to their children and reduce the incidence of father absence in the lives of children.

The third finding of the 1996 welfare reform law (P.L. 104-193) states: "Promotion of responsible fatherhood and motherhood is integral to successful child rearing and the well-being of children." Moreover, three of the four goals of the Temporary Assistance for Needy Families (TANF) program are consistent with the components of most fatherhood programs. The three fatherhood-related goals are: ending welfare dependence by employment and marriage; reducing out-of-wedlock pregnancies; and encouraging the formation and maintenance of two-parent families. Thus, states may spend TANF and TANF state Maintenance of Effort (MOE) funds on fatherhood programs. Further, any services that are directed to the goal of reducing nonmarital births or the goal of encouraging two-parent families are free of income eligibility rules.

With the exception of the federal Child Support Enforcement (CSE) program, fathers historically have been ignored with regard to their input or participation in welfare programs.

Moreover, it was not until 1996 that Congress broadened its view to acknowledge the non-economic contributions that fathers make to their children by authorizing the use of CSE funds to promote access and visitation programs. With the enactment of the 1996 welfare reform law, which helped reduce the welfare rolls, increase the employment of low-income mothers, and strengthen the CSE program, Congress began focusing its attention on the emotional well-being of children. Historically, Congress had treated visitation and child support as legally separate issues, with only child support enforcement activities under the purview of the federal government. The 1996 law authorized an annual $10 million entitlement of CSE funds to states to establish and operate access and visitation programs.[3]

It appears that a consensus has occurred regarding the need to connect or reconnect noncustodial parents to their children. During the 106th Congress, Representative Nancy Johnson, then chair of the Ways and Means Subcommittee on Human Resources, stated, "To take the next step in welfare reform we must find a way to help children by providing them with more than a working mother and sporadic child support." She noted that many low-income fathers have problems similar to those of mothers on welfare — namely, they are likely to have dropped out of high school, to have little work experience, and to have significant barriers that lessen their ability to find and/or keep a job. She also asserted that in many cases these men are "dead broke" rather than "dead beats" and that the federal government should help these noncustodial fathers meet both their financial and emotional obligations to their children.

> While fathers must fulfill their financial commitments, they must also fulfill their emotional commitments. Dads play indispensable roles that cannot be measured in dollars and cents: nurturer, mentor, disciplinarian, moral instructor, and skills coach, among other roles.
>
> Source: Executive Office of the President, A Blueprint for New Beginnings — A Responsible Budget for America's Priorities (Feb. 2001), chap. 12, p. 75.

During the 106th, 107th, and 108th Congresses, legislation was passed by the House but not by the Senate that would have established categorical competitive grants to community and faith-based organizations for responsible fatherhood programs. Moreover, each of President Bush's budgets has included grant programs for responsible fatherhood programs to help reconnect noncustodial parents to their children by providing job-related services to them and by improving their parenting and social interaction skills. During the period from 2002-2004, the responsible fatherhood bills that were passed by the House were part of welfare reauthorization legislation. The 109th Congress introduced several welfare reauthorization bills that included funding for responsible fatherhood grant programs. P.L. 109-171 — the Deficit Reduction Act of 2005 (S. 1932; H.Rept. 109-362) — which was enacted on February 8, 2006, included a provision that provides up to $50 million per year (FY2006-FY2010) for competitive responsible fatherhood grants. (For a more detailed legislative history of fatherhood initiatives, see the discussion of Legislative Action later in this article.)

WHAT ARE FATHERHOOD INITIATIVES?

The realization that one parent, especially a low-income parent, often cannot meet the financial needs of her or his children is not new. In 1975, Congress viewed the CSE program as a way to make noncustodial parents responsible for the financial support of their children. In more recent years, Congress has viewed the CSE program as the link that could enable single parents who are low-wage earners to become self-supporting. With the advent of welfare reform in 1996, Congress agreed that many noncustodial parents were in the same financial straits as the mothers of their children who were receiving cash welfare. Thus, the 1996 welfare reform law (P.L. 104-193) requires states to have laws under which the state has the authority to issue an order or request that a court or administrative process issue an order that requires noncustodial parents who were unable to pay their child support obligation for a child receiving TANF benefits to participate in TANF work activities. As noted earlier, the 1996 law also provided funding for states to develop programs that supported the noncustodial parent's right and responsibility to visit and interact with his or her children.

To help fathers and mothers meet their parental responsibilities, many policy analysts and observers support broad-based collaborative strategies that go beyond welfare and child support agencies and include schools, work programs, prison systems, churches, community organizations, and the health care system.

Although Congress only recently authorized federal funding specifically earmarked for responsible fatherhood programs, many states and localities, private organizations, and nonprofit agencies have been operating fatherhood programs for several years.[4] Most fatherhood programs include media campaigns that emphasize the importance of emotional, physical, psychological, and financial connections of fathers to their children. To counterbalance some of the procedural, psychological, emotional, and physical barriers to paternal involvement, most fatherhood programs include many of the following components:

- Parenting education — a course that describes the responsibilities of parents to their children; it discusses the need for affection, gentle guidance, financial support; the need to be a proud example and respectful of the child's mother; and the need to recognize developmentally appropriate behavior for children of different ages and respond appropriately to children's developmental needs;
- responsible decision-making (with regard to sexuality, establishment of paternity, and financial support);
- mentoring relationships with successful fathers and successful couples;
- mediation services (communicating with the other parent, supervised visitation, discipline of children, etc.);
- providing an understanding of the CSE program;
- conflict resolution, coping with stress, problem-solving skills;
- developing values in children, appropriate discipline, participation in child-rearing;
- understanding male-female relationships;
- peer support;
- practical tasks to stimulate involvement — discussing ways to increase parent-child interactions such as fixing dinner for children, taking children to the park, playing a

game, helping children with school work, listening to children's concerns, setting firm limits on behavior; and

- job training opportunities (skills development, interviewing skills, job search, job retention skills, job advancement skills, etc.).

Although most people refer to programs that seek to help fathers initiate or maintain contact with their children and become emotionally involved in their lives as "fatherhood" programs, the programs generally are gender-neutral. Their underlying goal is participation of the noncustodial parent in the lives of his or her children.

Funding

For FY2001, Congress appropriated $3 million for a nongovernmental national fatherhood organization named the National Fatherhood Initiative (P.L. 106-553), and an additional $500,000 for the National Fatherhood Initiative and $500,000 for another non-governmental organization called the Institute for Responsible Fatherhood and Family Revitalization (P.L. 106-554). However, the House and Senate failed to reach agreement on H.R. 4678 in the 106th Congress, a bill that included funding for a nationwide fatherhood grants program ($140 million over four years). Similarly, during the 107th and 108th Congress the House and the Senate did not reach agreement on legislation that included a responsible fatherhood grant program.

Nevertheless, several sources of federal funding for fatherhood programs already existed and continue to exist. They include the TANF program, TANF state Maintenance-of-Effort (MOE) funding, welfare-to-work funds, CSE funds, and Social Services Block Grant (Title XX) funds.[5] According to HHS, about half of all states use TANF funds for responsible fatherhood programs.[6] In addition, many private foundations are providing financial support for fatherhood programs.

As mentioned earlier, states can use TANF block grant funds and state MOE funds on programs or services that accomplish the broad purposes of the TANF program. These sources of funding are potentially the largest sources of funding for fatherhood initiatives.[7] Pursuant to P.L.109-171, the TANF block grant program to states was reauthorized through FY2010 at a funding level of $16.5 billion annually. In addition, the state funding or MOE requirement (at the 75% level) is about $10.4 billion.[8]

The cash welfare caseload declined from a peak of 5.0 million Aid to Families with Dependent Children (AFDC) families in 1995 to 1.9 million TANF families in 2005. The 62% reduction in the cash welfare caseload, together with the fixed block grant funding, means that funds that otherwise would have been spent for cash assistance are now available for other purposes. These other purposes could include fatherhood initiatives, which are allowable uses of TANF and state MOE funds. Moreover, fatherhood initiatives are not subject to the requirements that apply to spending for ongoing cash assistance such as work requirements and time limits.[9]

P.L. 109-171, the Deficit Reduction Act of 2005 (S. 1932; H.Rept. 109-362), was enacted during the 109th Congress. It included a provision that provides up to $50 million per year (for each of the five fiscal years 2006 through 2010) for competitive responsible fatherhood grants to states, territories, Indian tribes and tribal organizations, and public and nonprofit community organizations, including religious organizations, for responsible fatherhood initiatives.

According to data from the Administration for Children and Families (ACF) in the U.S. Department of Health and Human Services (HHS), 99 grantees were awarded 5-year contracts to implement responsible fatherhood programs. The contracts (in aggregate) amounted to $41 million per year.[10]

RESEARCH AND EVALUATION

Research findings indicate that father absence affects outcomes for children, in terms of schooling, emotional and behavioral maturity, labor force participation, and nonmarital childbearing. These findings hold when income is taken into account, so the negative effects of father absence are not limited to those created by reduced family income.[11]

Both advocates and critics of the CSE program agree that parents should be responsible for the economic and emotional well-being of their children. They agree that many low-income noncustodial parents are unable to meet their financial responsibility to their children and are barely able, or unable, to support themselves. They also agree that some noncustodial parents do not know how to be responsible parents because they were not taught that knowledge or were not exposed to enough positive role models that they could emulate. Below are several examples of demonstration programs that seek to, or sought to, help low-income men become responsible fathers by helping them to gain employment or job mobility and by teaching them life skills so that they might reconnect with their children in a positive sustained manner.

MDRC Parents' Fair Share Demonstration Project

The Parents' Fair Share (PFS) Demonstration was a national demonstration project that combined job training and placement, peer support groups, and other services with the goal of increasing the earnings and child support payments of unemployed noncustodial parents (generally fathers) of children on welfare, improving their parenting and communication skills, and providing an opportunity for them to participate more fully and effectively in the lives of their children.[12]

Between 1994 and 1996, over 5,000 noncustodial parents who were eligible to participate in the seven-site PFS demonstration were randomly assigned to either a program (experiment) group that would receive PFS services or a control group that would not receive PFS services. The interim report on the PFS demonstration, which was designed by MDRC and conducted and funded by public and private organizations, found that parents who received PFS services were more likely to pay child support through the CSE system than those who remained in the control group. In all seven sites, the proportion of parents who paid child support during the 18-month follow-up period increased significantly; but the amount of child support paid over the 18 months increased by a statistically significant amount in only two of the seven sites.

The final report on the PFS demonstration concluded that the program did not significantly increase employment or earnings among the full sample of PFS participants during the two years after they entered the program. However, the program did increase earnings among a subgroup of men who were characterized as "less employable" (i.e., those without a high school diploma and with little recent work experience).[13] In addition, another of the final reports found that although PFS did not affect the frequency of fathers' visits with their children, it did increase the level of disagreement between parents about child-rearing. According to the researchers, this finding might suggest that some noncustodial parents were becoming more involved in new areas of decision-making about the child, which the researchers viewed as a positive development. The report noted that the increased level of disagreements between the parents was not accompanied by an increased level of aggressive forms of conflict or domestic violence which researchers surmise might indicate that the parents were able to distinguish between legitimate parental differences of opinion versus latent animosity in their male-female relationship.[14]

One of the reports noted the following as lessons learned from the PFS demonstration.

> Low-income noncustodial fathers are a disadvantaged group. Many live on the edge of poverty and face severe barriers to finding jobs, while those who can find work typically hold low-wage or temporary jobs. Despite their low, irregular income, many of these fathers are quite involved in their children's lives and, when they can, provide financial and other kinds of support.... Some services, such as peer support proved to be very important and valuable to the men and became the focal point of the program. Other services, such as skill-building, were hard to implement because the providers had little experience working with such a disadvantaged group; it was difficult to find employers willing to hire the men, and the providers were not equipped to deal with the circumstances of men who often were simply trying to make it from one day to the next. Finally, we learned about the challenges of implementing a program like PFS, which involves the partnership of various agencies with different goals, and about the difficulty of recruiting low-income fathers into such a program.[15]

Some of the recommendations for future programs included structure the program to encourage longer-term participation and to include job retention services; provide fathers who cannot find private sector employment with community service jobs; earmark adequate funding for employment services, involve custodial mothers in the program and provide fathers with legal services to help them gain visitation rights; and encourage partnerships between CSE agencies and fatherhood programs.[16]

Some researchers of the PFS approach contend that a broader array of intensive employment services, such as skills training combined with part-time work and community service employment for persons who were unable to get job, might have improved the outcomes of the program. Other analysts maintain that most of the fathers who participated in the PFS demonstration were estranged from their children when they entered the program and that some of them participated in lieu of serving time in jail. They assert that new unwed fathers are generally very attached to their children around the time of the child's birth and probably are more motivated than fathers of older children to take advantage of the opportunities and/or services offered by fatherhood programs.[17]

Fragile Families and Child Well-Being Study

A "fragile" family consists of low-income children born outside of marriage whose two natural parents are working together to raise them — either by living together or frequent visitation. According to the 1997 National Survey of America's Families (NSAF), 25% of poor children under the age of two who were born outside of marriage lived with both of their biological parents; another 35% lived with their mother and saw their father at least every week.[18]

The Fragile Families and Child Well-being Study is designed to sample new births in 20 U.S. cities.[19] The study began in January 1997 and was scheduled to end in June 2004. The total sample size is 4,700 families, including 3,600 unmarried couples and 1,100 married couples. The data will be representative of nonmarital births in each of the 20 cities, and they also will be representative of all nonmarital births in U.S. cities with populations over 200,000. Follow-up interviews with both parents are scheduled for when the child is 12, 36, and 60 months-old to collect data on the child's health and development. The study is expected to provide previously unavailable information on questions such as the following:

- What are the conditions and capabilities of new unwed parents, especially fathers? How many of these men hold steady jobs? How many want to be involved in raising their children?
- What is the nature of the relationship between unwed parents? How many couples are involved in stable, long-term relationships? How many expect to marry? How many experience high levels of conflict or domestic violence?
- What factors push new unwed parents together? What factors pull them apart? How do public policies affect parents' behaviors and living arrangements?
- What are the long term consequences for parents, children, and society of new welfare regulations, stronger paternity establishment, and stricter child support enforcement? What roles do child care and health care policies play? How do these policies play out in different labor market environments?[20]

Initial analysis of the baseline data collected in 16 of the 20 cities from April 1998 through August 2000 indicate that 51% of unmarried parents live together (i.e., are cohabiting), and another 31% are romantically involved with each other. Further, 74% of the participant mothers said that they expect to marry the baby's father. The data also indicate that 30% of fathers had earnings of less than $10,500 per year, and 62% of mothers had earnings of less than $10,000 per year; about 43% of the mothers and 38% of the fathers lacked a high school degree. Although the data indicated that 85% of mothers and 98% of fathers worked at some point during the past year, 20% of fathers said that they were out of work during the week before the interview. The initial analysis also showed that 39% of the mothers drank alcohol, used drugs, or smoked during their pregnancies.[21]

Office of Child Support Enforcement (OCSE) Responsible Fatherhood Programs

The federal Office of Child Support Enforcement (OCSE) provided $2.0 million to fund Responsible Fatherhood demonstrations under Section 1115 of the Social Security Act. The programs operated in eight states between September 1997 and December 2002. The following eight states received Section 1115 grants or waivers from OCSE/Administration for Children and Families (ACF) to implement and test responsible fatherhood programs: California, Colorado, Maryland, Massachusetts, Missouri, New Hampshire, Washington, and Wisconsin. These projects attempted to improve the employment and earnings of under- and unemployed noncustodial parents, and to motivate them to become more financially and emotionally involved in the lives of their children. Although the projects shared common goals, they varied with respect to service components and service delivery. OCSE also provided about $500,000 for an evaluation of the demonstration projects. A report on the implementation of the programs (from initial start-up in late 1997 through December 1999) noted the following:

> The success of the Responsible Fatherhood Demonstration Projects appears to be tied to the commitment of the staff. Reaching alienated and disenfranchised populations and convincing them to change their attitudes and behaviors is hard work. It takes time, persistence, repeated contacts, fast action, patience, firmness, and endless resourcefulness. Programs need to recruit key program staff who are inspired and inspiring. They also need to be knowledgeable about community services in order to maximize opportunities for participants. First-hand knowledge is key. The best referrals are not made out of directories, but result from long-standing familiarity with community services, eligibility requirements, available resources, and relevant personnel. Dedicated, knowledgeable, and energetic staff can better counsel and steer parents into a course of action that makes them more financially and emotionally responsible for their children.[22]

A second, outcome report on the programs found that (1) low-income noncustodial fathers are a difficult population to recruit and serve; (2) many of the participants found jobs with the programs' help, but they were low-paying jobs and relatively few of the participants were able to increase earnings enough to meet their financial needs and those of their children; (3) child access problems were hard to define and resolve, and that mediation should be used more extensively; (4) child support guidelines result in orders for low-income noncustodial parents that are unrealistically high; (5) CSE agencies should collaborate with fatherhood programs and pursue routine enforcement activities, as well as adopt policies and incentives that are responsive to low-income fathers; and (6) criminal history was the norm rather than the exception among the program participants, many participants faced ongoing alcohol and substance abuse problems, many did not have reliable transportation, and many lacked a court-ordered visitation arrangement.[23]

On a more positive note, the outcome report found that employment rates and earnings increased significantly especially for noncustodial parents who were previously unemployed. In addition, child support compliance rates increased significantly especially for those who had not been paying previously. Moreover, the report found that 27% of the fathers reported seeing their children more often after completion of the program.

Partners for Fragile Families Demonstration

HHS has an ongoing partnership with the private-sector initiative called Partners for Fragile Families (PFF). The Partners for Fragile Families Project is an initiative of the National Center for Strategic Nonprofit Planning and Community Leadership (NPCL), a nonprofit organization based in Washington, D.C. The PFF was designed to help poor single fathers pull themselves out of poverty and build stronger links to their children and their children's mothers. The PFF was established in 1996 to provide support for these "fragile families," which are defined as low-income, never-married parents and their children. Research indicated that although many of the fathers in these families are involved with their children during the early childhood years, this involvement tends to diminish over time, often with negative consequences for the children. The PFF initiative is aimed at helping fathers work with the mothers of their children in sharing the legal, financial, and emotional responsibilities of parenthood.

In March 2000, HHS approved ten state waivers for the three-year Partners for Fragile Families Demonstration projects. The demonstration projects sought to develop new ways for CSE agencies and community-based nonprofit and faith-based organizations to work together to help young noncustodial fathers obtain employment, health, and social services; make child support payments to their children; learn parenting skills; and enable then to work with the mothers of their children to build stronger parenting partnerships. The demonstration project sites were located in California, Colorado, Illinois, Indiana, Maryland, Massachusetts, Minnesota, New York, Pennsylvania, and Wisconsin.[24] According to HHS, of the $9.7 million in federal funding budgeted for the projects, $7.1 million was spent. An additional $1.4 million was spent for an evaluation of the projects.

ISSUES

An underlying tension in the debate on fatherhood initiatives is the concern of some women's and mothers' rights groups, such as the National Women's Law Center and the National Organization for Women (NOW), that an emphasis on the importance of fathers may lead to undervaluing single-parent families maintained by mothers, that services for fathers may be at the expense of services for mothers, and that the "pro-fatherhood" discourse might give fathers' rights groups some leverage in challenging child custody, child support, and visitation arrangements. Some analysts contend that the policy debate on fatherhood initiatives must be based on the view that the welfare of fathers, mothers, and children are intertwined and interdependent; otherwise, the debate will be very divisive and unproductive.[25]

Many issues are associated with the federal government's support of fatherhood initiatives. A few examples are Is the goal of federal policy to promote and support the involvement of fathers in their children's lives regardless of the father's relationship with the children's mother? What if the father has children by more than one woman? What is the federal policy with regard to incarcerated parents and parents recently released from prison? Does the federal government support counseling, education, and supervised visitation for abusive fathers so that they can reconnect with their children?

The discussion below examines two issues that will likely impact the success of congressional fatherhood initiatives. The first deals with the role of the CSE agency in fatherhood programs. Presently, the CSE program is the starting place for many fatherhood programs. Some analysts contend that since many noncustodial parents have a negative view of the CSE program, the use of the CSE program to recruit fathers does not bode well for the success of such programs. Several of the fatherhood bills would make competitive grants available to community organizations and other groups that have experience in working with low-income men. Many of the fatherhood bills introduced in recent Congresses included evaluation components. The second issue examines father involvement in the context of the father's relationship to the child's mother. The second issue is based on the premise that formal marital relationships last longer and are more conducive to long-term interaction between fathers and children than other types of relationships.

CSE System and Noncustodial Parents Often at Odds

During the period FY1978-FY2006, child support payments collected by the CSE agencies increased from $1 billion to $23.9 billion. Moreover, the program has made significant improvements in other program measures as well, such as the number of parents located, paternities established, and child support orders established. Advocates of the CSE program say that this dramatic program performance is aside from the indirect and intangible benefits of the program, such as increased personal responsibility and welfare cost-avoidance. Critics of the CSE program contend that even with an unprecedented array of "big brother" enforcement tools such as license (professional, driver's, recreational) and passport revocation, seizure of banking accounts, retirement funds, and lottery winnings, and automatic income withholding from pay checks, the program still collects only 19% of child support obligations for which it has responsibility and collects payments for only 54% of its caseload.

Although the CSE program has historically been the policy answer to the problem of father absence, because its focus until recently was exclusively on financial support, it has had the practical effect of alienating many low-income fathers who are unable to meet their child support obligations. Some policy analysts maintain that fathers are in effect devalued when their role in their children's lives is based solely on their cash contributions. They argue that public policies are needed to support the father's role as nurturer, disciplinarian, mentor, and moral instructor.[26]

Information obtained from noncustodial fathers for various surveys and studies consistently tells the same story. Not surprisingly, noncustodial parents, especially low-income fathers, prefer informal child support agreements between themselves and the child's mother wherein they contribute cash support when they can and provide noncash aid such as taking care of the children from time to time and buying food, clothing, presents, etc. as often as they can. Many noncustodial fathers maintain that the CSE system is dismissive of their financial condition and continues to pursue child support payments (current as well as arrearages) even when it knows that many of them can barely support themselves. They argue that for welfare families, the CSE program generally does not improve their child's well-being because their child support payments are used to benefit the state and federal government (i.e., welfare reimbursement) rather than their child. They contend that the CSE program causes conflicts between them and their child's mother because the women often use it as leverage by threatening to report them to CSE authorities, take them back to court, have more of their wages garnished, or have them arrested.[27]

Many observers maintain that noncustodial parents and the CSE program have irreconcilable differences and that the most that should be expected is for the noncustodial parent to clearly understand the purposes of the CSE program, the requirements imposed on the custodial parent, the noncustodial parents' rights to have their child support payments modified if they incur a financial change in circumstances, and that they as noncustodial parents have a moral and societal responsibility to have (to build) a loving relationship with their children.[28] If the CSE program continues to be the entrance to fatherhood programs, most observers contend that the fact that the CSE program has not been effective in gaining the cooperation and trust of many noncustodial parents must be acknowledged and addressed. Several analysts suggest that to be successful, fatherhood programs may need to operate independently of the formal CSE system.

Others assert that more than any other agency of state government, the CSE program has the responsibility and is in the position to reach out to fathers who need supportive services. They state that CSE agencies are already involved in forging relationships with fathers through partnerships with community-based organizations. They also note that CSE agencies provide a natural link to coordinate with TANF agencies to help families achieve self-sufficiency.[29]

Although we do not have any evaluations on the effectiveness of fatherhood programs delivered through a CSE framework versus fatherhood programs that place little emphasis on the formal CSE system, all of the fatherhood bills introduced in the 107th and 108th Congresses included funding for evaluation, and so did many of the fatherhood bills in the 109th Congress. (Readers should note that P.L. 109-171 does not include funding for the evaluation of responsible fatherhood grant programs.)

Noncustodial Father Involvement vs. Promotion of Marriage vs. Maintenance of Fragile Families

The first finding of the 1996 welfare reform law is that marriage is the foundation of a successful society. The second finding is that marriage is an essential institution of a successful society which promotes the interests of children.[30] However, some child welfare advocates argue that marriage is not necessarily the best alternative for all women and their children. It is generally agreed that single-parent families are a better alternative for children than living with an abusive father. Many observers caution that government must be careful about supporting programs that provide cash incentives to induce people to marry or that coerce people into marrying. They note the problems associated with child-bride marriages and the short-term and often unhappy nature of the so-called "shot gun" marriage. Others respond that many long-lasting marriages were based on financial alliances (e.g., to increase economic status, family wealth, status in the community, etc.). They also point out that most government programs are sensitive to the issues of domestic violence and include supports to prevent or end such actions.

Many young children live with both of their parents who are not married but who are cohabiting. Noting this, some analysts argue that coercive policies designed to promote certain types of family structures (e.g., nuclear families) at the expense of others may undermine nontraditional family relationships. They contend that more emphasis should be placed on trying to meet the needs of these fragile families to enable them to stay together for longer periods of time. They maintain that if these parents wanted to be married they would be married.[31] They also point out that because of the complexity of many family relationships, there are no easy answers. A single-focus policy, no matter whether it aims to support traditional family relationships or fragile families, can place children in less desirable situations. For instance, promoting marriage of biological parents may result in supporting situations where some children in the household have a stepparent if all the children are not from the same union. Similarly, promoting fragile families also could result in supporting situations where a biological parent is absent if all of the children in the household are not all from the same union.

Some pro-marriage analysts point out that about 75% of children born to cohabiting parents will see their parents separate before they reach age 16, compared to about 33% of those born to married parents. Some observers note that even with supports it is unlikely that fragile families (unmarried couple) will remain together as long as married families. Thus, they argue that the promotion of marriage should be incorporated into fatherhood programs if the goal is lifetime involvement of fathers in the lives of their children.

In contrast, fatherhood initiatives are sometimes viewed as incompatible with initiatives that encourage the formation and maintenance of two-parent families, and with initiatives that promote marriage. In fact, many observers argue that the focus should be the participation of fathers in their children's lives, regardless of the marital status of the parents. As mentioned earlier, the TANF law states that the second purpose of the block grant is to "end the dependence of needy parents on government benefits by promoting job preparation, work, and marriage." The fourth purpose of the TANF block grant is to "encourage the formation and maintenance of two-parent families." There has been some discussion about whether the fourth purpose means married-couple families or just two parents who are involved in their children's lives, regardless of whether they are married or even living together. In late 1999, the Clinton Administration issued A Guide on Funding for Children and Families through the TANF program which broadly interpreted two-parent families to mean not only married-couple families, but also never-married, separated, and divorced parents, whether living together or not. Thus, many states classify their fatherhood programs and programs that encourage visitation by noncustodial parents under the rubric of fulfilling the purposes of the TANF program.[32]

In addition, it should be noted that some research indicates that there may be a racial component in the marriage promotion versus fatherhood involvement debate.

In 2005, 69.5% of black births were to unmarried women, whereas only 25.4% of white births were to unmarried women. Given this demographic reality of black and white families in the U.S., the authors of the study[33] contend that proposals that earmark five times as much money for marriage promotion as for responsible fatherhood promotion[34] seem "racially insensitive." (Readers should note that P.L. 109-171 funds marriage promotion grants at twice the amount of responsible fatherhood grants (i.e., $100 million per year for five years versus $50 million per year for five years).

LEGISLATIVE ACTION

During the 106th Congress, President Clinton's FY2001 budget included $255 million for the first year of a proposed "Fathers Work/Families Win" initiative to help low-income noncustodial parents and low-income working families work and support their children. The "Fathers Work/Families Win" initiative would have been administered by the Department of Labor (DoL). The "Fathers Work" component ($125 million) would have been limited to noncustodial parents (primarily fathers) and the "Families Win" component ($130 million) would have been targeted more generally to low-income families.

The proposed "Fathers Work" grant program was designed to help low-income noncustodial parents who were not living with their children carry out their financial and emotional responsibilities to their children. The proposed "Families Win" grant program was designed to help "hard-pressed" working families obtain the supports and skills they need to get a job and succeed in the job and avoid TANF assistance. These funds were intended to leverage existing resources to help families retain jobs and upgrade skills and get connected to critical work supports, such as child care, child support, health care, food stamps, earned income tax credit, housing, and transportation. Neither the House nor Senate FY2001 appropriations bill (H.R. 4577, 106th Congress) for the Departments of Labor, Health and Human Services, and Education, and Related Agencies included funding for the Fathers Work/Families Win proposal.

From the beginning of his presidency, President Bush has indicated his support for responsible fatherhood initiatives. President Bush's FY2002 budget (issued in February 2001, 107th Congress) proposed $64 million in 2002 ($315 million over five years) to strengthen the role of fathers in the lives of families. This initiative would have provided competitive grants to faith-based and community organizations that help unemployed or low-income fathers and their families avoid or leave cash welfare, as well as to programs that promote successful parenting and strengthen marriage. The initiative also would have funded projects of national significance that support expansion of state and local responsible fatherhood efforts.

President Bush's FY2003 budget proposed $20 million (for FY2003) for competitive grants to community and faith-based organizations for programs that help noncustodial fathers support their families to avoid or leave cash welfare, become more involved in their children's lives, and promote successful parenting and encourage and support healthy marriages and married fatherhood.

President Bush's FY2004 budget proposed $20 million annually (for FY2004-FY2008) for promotion and support of responsible fatherhood and healthy marriage. The funding was expected to promote and support involved, committed, and responsible fatherhood and encourage the formation and stability of healthy marriages. The FY2004 budget proposal also would have increased the annual funding of the CSE access and visitation grant program gradually from $10 million annually to $20 million annually by FY2007.

President Bush's FY2005 budget proposed $50 million (for FY2005) for 75 competitive grants to faith-based and community organizations, together with Indian tribes and tribal organizations, to encourage and help fathers to support their families, avoid welfare, improve fathers' ability to manage family business affairs, and support healthy marriages and married fatherhood.

President Bush's FY2006 budget proposed $40 million (for FY2006) for a grant program to public and nonprofit community organizations, including religious organizations, and Indian tribes and tribal organizations, for demonstration service projects to help noncustodial fathers become more involved in their children's lives and to encourage and support healthy marriages between parents raising children.

President Bush's FY2007 budget proposed $100 million for competitive matching grants to states for marriage promotion. It also included the $150 million for healthy marriage and responsible fatherhood programs that was included in P.L. 109-171 as part of welfare reauthorization. As noted in this article, pursuant to P.L. 109-171, $50 million is specifically allocated for responsible fatherhood programs.

President Bush's FY2008 budget included the $150 million for healthy marriage and responsible fatherhood programs that was included in P.L. 109-171 as part of welfare reauthorization. As noted, pursuant to P.L. 109-171, $50 million is specifically allocated for responsible fatherhood programs.

106th Congress

During the 106th Congress, legislation was twice passed by the House (but not acted on by the Senate — H.R. 3073, the proposed Fathers Count Act of 1999, and H.R. 4678, the proposed Child Support Distribution Act of 2000) that would have authorized funding ($140 million over five years in H.R. 3073 and million over four years in H.R. 4678) to establish a program (usually referred $140 to as fatherhood initiatives) to make grants to public or private entities for projects designed to promote marriage, promote successful parenting and the involvement of fathers in the lives of their children, and help fathers improve their economic status by providing job-related services to them.

107th Congress

During the 107th Congress, several bills (H.R. 1300/S. 653, H.R. 1471, S. 685, S. 940/H.R. 1990, H.R. 2893, H.R. 3625, H.R. 4090[35], S. 2524, and H.R. 4737) that included fatherhood initiatives were introduced, but none were enacted.

The purposes of the fatherhood programs in the bills introduced generally were the same: fatherhood programs must be designed to promote marriage through counseling, mentoring, and other activities; promote successful parenting through counseling, providing information about good parenting practices including payment of child support, and other activities; and help noncustodial parents and their families avoid or leave cash welfare by providing work-first services, job training, subsidized employment, career-advancing education, and other activities.

However, the structure of the fatherhood programs differed. For example, H.R. 4737 as amended and passed by the House would have added a new part C to Title IV of the Social Security Act to provide competitive grants to public and private entities to operate an array of fatherhood programs. The competitive grants would have been administered by the Department of Health and Human Services (HHS). The appropriation amount for the fatherhood grants was set at $20 million a year for each of the five fiscal years FY2003 through FY2007; up to 15% of the annual appropriation was to be available for the cost of various demonstration projects and evaluations of the competitive grants.

In contrast, H.R. 4737 as amended in the nature of a substitute by the Senate Finance Committee appeared to have more of an emphasis on helping low-income noncustodial parents find and retain work. It would have amended part D of title IV of the Social Security Act (i.e., the Child Support section) to provide grants to states to (1) establish a noncustodial parent employment grant program and (2) conduct policy reviews and develop recommendations, and conduct demonstration projects with the goals of obtaining and retaining employment for low-income noncustodial parents, increasing child support payments, increasing the involvement of low-income noncustodial parents with their children, and coordinating services for low-income noncustodial parents. The HHS Secretary and the Secretary of Labor would have jointly awarded grants to eligible states for the purpose of establishing, in coordination with counties and other local governments, supervised employment programs for noncustodial parents who have a history of irregular payment or nonpayment of child support obligations and who are determined to be in need of employment services in order to pay their child support obligations. The appropriation amount for the noncustodial parent employment program was set at $25 million a year for each of the four fiscal years FY2004 through FY2007. The appropriation amount for the grants, administered by the HHS Secretary, to states for policy reviews, recommendations, and demonstration projects also was set at $25 million a year for each of the four fiscal years FY2004 through FY2007.

Although H.R. 4737, amended, was passed by the House on May 16, 2002 (H.Rept. 107-460, Part 1), and reported favorably in the nature of a substitute by the Senate Finance Committee (S.Rept. 107-221) on July 25, 2002, it was not passed by the full Senate.

108th Congress

The 108th Congress introduced several bills that included responsible fatherhood provisions (i.e., S. 5, S. 448, S. 604, and S. 657, S. 1443, and S. 2830; H.R. 4 and H.R. 936). None of the bills became law.

On February 13, 2003, the House passed H.R. 4 (108th Congress), a welfare reauthorization bill (that was essentially identical to H.R. 4737 as passed by the House in 2002) that would have provided $20 million per year for each of FY2004-FY2008 for a responsible fatherhood grant program.

On September 10, 2003, the Senate Finance Committee approved its version of H.R. 4 (S.Rept. 108-162), which would have established a $75 million responsible fatherhood program composed of four components for each of the fiscal years 2004-2008: (1) a $20 million grant program for up to 10 eligible states to conduct demonstration programs; (2) a $30 million grant for eligible entities to conduct demonstration programs; (3) $5 million for a nationally recognized nonprofit fatherhood promotion organization to develop and promote a responsible fatherhood media campaign; and (4) a $20 million block grant for states to conduct responsible fatherhood media campaigns. Although H.R. 4 was debated on the Senate floor during the period March 29-April 1, 2004, consideration of the bill was not completed when a motion to limit debate on the bill failed to garner the needed 60 votes. The Senate did not bring the bill back to the floor before the end of the session.

During the period from 2002-2004, the responsible fatherhood bills that were passed by the House were part of welfare reauthorization legislation. (The funding for the Temporary Assistance for Needy Families (TANF) block grant, mandatory child care, and the abstinence education block grant — which were part of the 1996 welfare reform legislation (P.L. 104-193) whose funding authority expired on September 30, 2002 — has continued under a number of temporary extension measures.)

109th Congress

The 109th Congress introduced several welfare reauthorization bills that included responsible fatherhood provisions (i.e., H.R. 240/S. 105, S. 6, and S. 667). S. 1932 (the Deficit Reduction Act of 2005) also included a provision that provided competitive grants for responsible fatherhood activities.

On January 4, 2005, a TANF reauthorization bill (H.R. 240) was introduced in the 109th Congress. It included provisions that authorized the HHS Secretary to make competitive grants totaling \$20 million for each of the fiscal years 2006 through 2010 to public and nonprofit community organizations, including religious organizations, and Indian tribes and tribal organizations for responsible fatherhood demonstration programs. The purposes of the fatherhood programs were to (1) promote responsible, caring and effective parenting and encouraging positive father involvement, including the positive involvement of nonresident fathers; (2) enhance the abilities and commitment of unemployed or low-income fathers to provide support for their families and to avoid or leave welfare; (3) improve fathers' ability to effectively manage family business affairs; and (4) encourage and support healthy marriages and married fatherhood. Not more than 15% of the annual appropriation would have been available for the costs of two multicity, multistate demonstration projects, projects of national significance that support expansion of state and local responsible fatherhood efforts, and an evaluation of the programs. The fatherhood provisions in H.R. 240 were identical to those that were included in H.R. 4 as passed by the House on February 13, 2003 (108th Congress). S. 105, which is identical to H.R. 240, was introduced in the Senate on January 24, 2005.

On January 24, 2005, another TANF reauthorization bill (S. 6) was introduced in the 109th Congress. It would have established a \$75 million responsible fatherhood program composed of four components for each of the fiscal years 2006-2010: (1) a \$20 million grant program for up to 10 eligible states to conduct demonstration programs; (2) a \$30 million grant for eligible entities to conduct demonstration programs; (3) \$5 million for a nationally recognized nonprofit fatherhood promotion organization to develop and promote a responsible fatherhood media campaign; and (4) a \$20 million block grant for states to conduct responsible fatherhood media campaigns. The purposes of the demonstration grants were to promote responsible fatherhood through (1) marriage promotion (through counseling, mentoring, disseminating information about the advantages of marriage and two-parent involvement for children, etc., (2) parenting activities (through counseling, mentoring, mediation, disseminating information about good parenting practices, etc.), and (3) fostering economic stability of fathers (through work first services, job search, job training, subsidized employment, education, etc.). The fatherhood provisions in S. 6 were identical to those that were included in H.R. 4 as passed by the Senate Finance Committee on October 3, 2003 (H.Rept. 108-162, 108th Congress).

On March 17, 2005, the Senate Finance Committee reported S. 667, a TANF reauthorization bill. It would have established a $76 million responsible fatherhood program composed of five components for each of the fiscal years 2006-2010. It would have (1) *appropriated* $20 million for a grant program for up to 10 eligible states to conduct demonstration programs; (2) *appropriated* $30 million for grants for eligible entities to conduct demonstration programs; (3) authorized $5 million for a nationally recognized nonprofit fatherhood promotion organization to develop and promote a responsible fatherhood media campaign; (4) authorized a $20 million block grant for states to conduct responsible fatherhood media campaigns; and (5) authorized $1 million for a nationally recognized nonprofit research and education fatherhood organization to establish a national resource center for responsible fatherhood. The fatherhood provisions in S. 667 were almost identical to those in S. 6, except that funding for the demonstration grants to states and eligible entities would have been assured because money was appropriated in the bill for those activities (S.Rept. 109-51, 109th Congress).

On December 19, 2005, the House passed the conference report on S. 1932, the Deficit Reduction Act of 2005 (H.Rept. 109-362). On December 21, the Senate passed the conference report on S. 1932 with amendments. The conference report was subsequently passed again by the House on February 1, 2006. On February 8, 2006, President Bush signed S. 1932 into P.L. 109-171. Among other things, P.L. 109-171 reauthorized the TANF block grant at $16.5 billion annually through FY2010 and included a provision that provides up to $50 million per year (for each of the five fiscal years 2006 through 2010) in competitive grants to states, territories, Indian tribes and tribal organizations, and public and nonprofit community organizations, including religious organizations, for responsible fatherhood initiatives.

Under P.L. 109-171, responsible fatherhood funds can be spent on activities to promote responsible fatherhood through (1) marriage promotion (through counseling, mentoring, disseminating information about the advantages of marriage and two-parent involvement for children, etc.), (2) parenting activities (through counseling, mentoring, mediation, disseminating information about good parenting practices, etc.), (3) fostering economic stability of fathers (through work first services, job search, job training, subsidized employment, education, etc.), or (4) contracting with a nationally recognized nonprofit fatherhood promotion organization to develop, promote, or distribute a media campaign to encourage the appropriate involvement of parents in the lives of their children, particularly focusing on responsible fatherhood; and/or to develop a national clearinghouse to help states and communities in their efforts to promote and support marriage and responsible fatherhood.

110th Congress

The 110th Congress has introduced one bill that includes responsible fatherhood provisions (S. 1626). Among other things, S. 1626, the proposed Responsible Fatherhood and Healthy Families Act of 2007 introduced by Senator Bayh, would increase funding for the responsible fatherhood grants (authorized by the Deficit Reduction Act of 2005, P.L. 109-171) from no more than $50 million per year for each of the fiscal years 2006-2010 to at least $100 million per year for those fiscal years.

REFERENCES

[1] U.S. Census Bureau. Family and Living Arrangements. *Table FM-1: Families, by Presence of Own Children Under 18: 1950-2004*. Internet Release Date: June 29, 2005. See [http://www.census.gov/population/socdemo/hh-fam/fm1.pdf].

[2] Sara McLanahan and Gary Sandefur, *Growing Up With a Single Parent: What Hurts, What Helps* (Cambridge, MA: Harvard University Press, 1994), see also L. Bumpass, "Children and Marital Disruption: A Replication and Update," *Demography*, vol. 21(1984), pp. 71-82; Rebecca A. Maynard, ed., *Kids Having Kids: A Robin Hood Foundation Special Report on the Costs of Adolescent Childbearing* (New York, 1996).

[3] The child access and visitation program (Section 391 of P.L. 104-193) funded the following activities in FY2005: mediation, counseling, parental education, development of parenting plans, visitation enforcement, monitored visitation, neutral dropoff and pickup, supervised visitation, and development of guidelines for visitation and custody. In FY2005, about 69,000 individuals received services. The most common services were parenting education, supervised visitation, and mediation. Most states used a mix of services. Most of the service providers were Human Services Agencies. Individuals were referred to services by the courts, CSE or welfare agencies, and others, as well as by self-referral. Services were both mandatory and voluntary, as determined by the state. Source: U.S. Department of Health and Human Services, Administration for Children and Families, Office of Child Support Enforcement, *State Child Access and Visitation Grants: State/Jurisdiction Profiles for FY2005* (Washington, April 2007).

[4] National Governors Association, *Promoting Responsible Fatherhood: An Update* (Washington, August 3, 1998).

[5] "Funding Sources for Fatherhood Programs," *Welfare Information Network*, vol. 5, no. 2 (January 2001).

[6] U.S. Department of Health and Human Services, *HHS Fact Sheet: Promoting Responsible Fatherhood* (Washington, April 26, 2002).

[7] In addition to long-term welfare recipients, the $2.7 billion in welfare-to-work funds appropriated for FY1998 and FY1999 could have been used to provide services for certain noncustodial parents who were unemployed, underemployed, or having difficulty making their child support payments. States and localities were allowed to continue to spend their welfare-to-work funds through FY2004.

[8] The TANF block grant program also has a MOE requirement that states continue to spend at least 75% (80% if they fail to meet TANF work requirements) of what they spent under prior law cash welfare-related programs in FY1994 on families that meet TANF eligibility requirements.

[9] Dana Reichert, *Broke but Not Deadbeat: Reconnecting Low-Income Fathers and Children* (Washington, National Conference of State Legislatures, July 1999).

[10] Information on the responsible fatherhood grants in each of the 10 HHS regions is available at [http://www.acf.hhs.gov/programs/ofa/hmabstracts/index.htm].

[11] Meeting the Challenge: What the Federal Government Can Do to Support Responsible Fatherhood Efforts — A Report to the President [...] (Washington, January 2001), [http:// fatherhood.hhs.gov/guidance01].

[12] The Parents' Fair Share (PFS) demonstration was funded by a consortium of private foundations (the Pew Charitable Trusts, the Ford Foundation, the AT and T Foundation, the McKnight Foundation, and the Northwest Area Foundation) and federal agencies (the U.S. Department of Human Services and the U.S. Department of Labor).The PFS demonstration was conducted in seven cities: Dayton, Ohio; Grand Rapids, Michigan; Jacksonville, Florida; Los Angeles, California; Memphis, Tennessee; Springfield, Massachusetts; and Trenton, New Jersey.

[13] John M. Martinez and Cynthia Miller, Working and Earning: The Impact of Parents' Fair Share on Low-Income Fathers' Employment (New York: MDRC, October 2000).

[14] Virginia Knox and Cindy Redcross, Parenting and Providing: The Impact of Parents' Fair Share on Paternal Involvement (New York: MDRC, October 2000).

[15] Cynthia Miller and Virginia Knox, The Challenge of Helping Low-Income Fathers Support Their Children: Final Lessons from Parents' Fair Share (New York: MDRC, November 2001), pp. v-vi.

[16] Ibid., p. v.

[17] Sara McLanahan, *Testimony before the Mayor's Task Force on Fatherhood Promotion,* National Fatherhood Summit, Washington, D.C., June 14, 1999.

[18] Elaine Sorensen, Ronald Mincy, and Ariel Halpern, *Redirecting Welfare Policy Toward Building Strong Families* (Washington: Urban Institute, March 2000).

[19] The Fragile Families and Child Well-being Study is supported by grants from the National Institute of Child Health and Human Development, and the Office of Population Research at Princeton University and by funding provided by: California Health Care Foundation, the Center for Research on Religion and Urban Civil Society at the University of Pennsylvania, Commonwealth Fund, Ford Foundation, Foundation for Child Development, Fund for New Jersey, William T. Grant Foundation, Healthcare Foundation of New Jersey, William and Flora Hewlett Foundation, Hogg Foundation, Christian A. Johnson Endeavor Foundation, Kronkosky Charitable Foundation, Leon Lowenstein Foundation, John D., and Catherine T. MacArthur Foundation, A.L. Mailman Family Foundation, Charles Stewart Mott Foundation, National Science Foundation, David and Lucile Packard Foundation, Public Policy Institute of California, Robert Wood Johnson Foundation, St. David's Hospital Foundation, St. Vincent Hospital and Health Services, and the U.S. Department of Health and Human Services.

[20] Irwin Garfinkel and Sara McLanahan, "Fragile Families and Child Well-Being: A Survey of New Parents," *Focus* (University of Wisconsin-Madison, Institute for Research on Poverty), vol. 21, no. 1 (spring 2000), pp. 9-11.

[21] Sara McLanahan, Irwin Garfinkel, Nancy E. Reichman, Julien Teitler, Marcia Carlson, and Christina Norland Audigier, *The Fragile Families and Child Wellbeing Study: Baseline Report* (Princeton: Bendheim-Thoman Center for Research on Child Wellbeing, August 2001; rev. March 2003), at [http://www.fragilefamilies.princeton.edu/].

[22] Jessica Pearson and Nancy Thoennes, with David Price and Jane Venohr, *OCSE Responsible Fatherhood Programs: Early Implementation Lessons* (Washington: U.S. Department of Health and Human Services, Administration for Children and Families, Center for Policy Research and Policy Studies, June 2000) p. 9.

[23] Jessica Pearson, Nancy Thoennes, and Lanae Davis, with Jane Venohr, David Price, and Tracy Griffith, *OCSE Responsible Fatherhood Programs: Client Characteristics*

and Program Outcomes (Washington: U.S. Department of Health and Human Services, Administration for Children and Families, Center for Policy Research and Policy Studies [HHS Contract No. 100-98-0015], September 2003).

[24] See [http://fatherhood.hhs.gov/index.shtml] and [http://www.npcl.org/program/pff.htm].

[25] William J. Doherty, Edward F. Kouneski, and Martha Farrell Erickson, *Responsible Fathering: An Overview and Conceptual Framework — Final Report* Washington, U.S. Department of Health and Human Services, Administration for Children and Families, Center for Policy Research and Policy Studies [HHS-100-93-0012], September 1996).

[26] Wade F. Horn and Isabel V. Sawhill, *Making Room for Daddy: Fathers, Marriage, and Welfare Reform,* Brookings Institution Working Paper (Washington, April 26, 2001), p. 4.

[27] Maureen Waller and Robert Plotnick, "A Failed Relationship? Low-Income Families and the Child Support Enforcement System," *Focus* (University of Wisconsin-Madison. Institute for Research on Poverty), vol. 21, no. 1 (spring 2000), pp. 12-17. See also *Family Ties: Improving Paternity Establishment Practices and Procedures for Low-Income Mothers, Fathers and Children* (Washington: National Women's Law Center and Center on Fathers, Families, and Public Policy, 2000), pp. 9-11.

[28] Waller and Plotnick,"A Failed Relationship?"

[29] National Child Support Enforcement Association, *Resolution on Fatherhood Initiatives*, adopted by the NCSEA Board of Directors on July 29, 2000, [http://www.ncsea.org/pdf/2000fatherhood.pdf].

[30] The majority of pre-TANF evaluations of welfare initiatives that examine family formation decisions have found little, if any, impact of state policies on decisions to marry. One recent exception is an evaluation of the Minnesota Family Investment Program (MFIP). In this program, compared to those who were subject to the AFDC requirements, more single-parent participants subject to new policies under MFIP got married and fewer of the two-parent participants had divorced within three years after the program began.

[31] See "Is Marriage a Viable Objective for Fragile Families?" *Fragile Families Research Brief 9* (Princeton: Bendheim-Thoman Center for Research on Child Wellbeing, July 2002).

[32] Wade Horn, "Wedding Bell Blues: Marriage and Welfare Reform," *Brookings Review,* summer 2001, pp. 40-41.

[33] Ronald B. Mincy and Chien-Chung Huang, *The M Word: The Rise and Fall of Interracial Coalitions on Fathers and Welfare Reform.* Bowling Green State University Working Paper 02-7 (February 25, 2002), pp. 1-5, 32.

[34] H.R. 4737 as passed by the House in the 107th Congress authorized \$100 million annually for five years for competitive matching grants that require a dollar-for-dollar match for marriage promotion activities, resulting in total funding of \$200 million annually for five years. Further, an additional \$100 million per year for five years was authorized for research and demonstration grants and technical assistance related to the healthy marriage promotion activities. In contrast, H.R. 4737 (107th Congress) authorized \$20 million annually for five years for responsible fatherhood grants.

[35] H.R. 4090, as amended, was ordered reported by the House Ways and Means Committee on May 2, 2002 (H.Rept. 107-460, Part 1). The bill would have provided

$20 million in grants per year for a five-year period (FY2003-FY2007) to public entities and nonprofit community entities, including religious organizations, and to Indian tribes and tribal organizations to promote responsible, caring and effective parenting and to encourage positive father involvement, including the positive involvement of nonresident fathers; enhance the abilities and commitment of unemployed or low-income fathers to provide support for their families and to avoid or leave welfare; improve fathers' ability to effectively manage family business affairs; and encourage and support healthy marriages and married fatherhood. Note: H.R. 4737, a bill that included identical "fatherhood" provisions, passed the House on May 16, 2002.

In: Families: Rights, Laws and Stability
Editors: J. R. Redmund, K. B. Killigan, pp. 75-94
ISBN: 978-1-60456-203-3

Chapter 4

INTERNATIONAL POPULATION ASSISTANCE AND FAMILY PLANNING PROGRAMS: ISSUES FOR CONGRESS*

Luisa Blanchfield

ABSTRACT

Since 1965, the U.S. government has supported international population planning based on principles of volunteerism and informed choice that gives participants access to information on all methods of birth control. This policy, however, has generated contentious debate for over two decades, resulting in frequent clarification and modification of U.S. international family planning programs. Given the divisive nature of this debate, U.S. funding of these programs will likely remain a point of contention during the 110th Congress.

In 1984, controversy arose over U.S. population aid policy when the Reagan Administration introduced restrictions, which became known as the "Mexico City policy." The Mexico City policy denies U.S. funds to foreign non-governmental organizations (NGOs) that perform or promote abortion as a method of family planning — even if the activities are undertaken with non-U.S. funds. Presidents Reagan and George H.W. Bush also banned grants to the U.N. Population Fund (UNFPA) due to evidence of coercive family planning practices in China.

President Clinton resumed UNFPA funding and reversed the Mexico City policy in 1993. President George W. Bush, however, re-applied the Mexico City restrictions. Following a State Department investigation of family planning programs in China, the Administration suspended U.S. contributions to UNFPA in 2002, citing violations of the "Kemp-Kasten" amendment, which bans U.S. assistance to organizations that support or participate in the management of coercive family planning programs. The suspension of U.S. contributions to UNFPA has continued through FY2007.

Foreign operations programs are currently being funded under the terms of a continuing resolution, which provides funding similar to the FY2006 level with some adjustments. Therefore, the current level of funding for bilateral family planning

---

* Excerpted from CRS Report RL33250, dated September 21, 2007.

activities should be around $440 million — the enacted level for bilateral population assistance activities in FY2006 (see H.R. 3057/P.L. 109-102).

The Bush Administration's FY2008 budget request includes $324.8 million for family planning health activities. The Administration proposed that $25 million in UNFPA funding be drawn from the $324.8 million bilateral family planning request if the organization is determined eligible under the Kemp-Kasten amendment.

On June 21, 2007, the House passed H.R. 2764, the State, Foreign Operations, and Related Appropriations Bill, FY2008, which appropriates $441 million for reproductive health and voluntary family planning programs, and $40 million for UNFPA if it is found eligible under the Kemp-Kasten amendment. On June 22, 2007, the Senate passed its version of H.R. 2764, which appropriated $461.06 million for family planning and reproductive health programs. It did not specify a funding amount for UNFPA.

U.S. Population Assistance Issues: Setting the Context

Overview

Population assistance became a global issue in the late 1950s and early 1960s after several private foundations, among them the International Planned Parenthood Federation (IPPF), began providing money to developing countries to control high population growth rates. In 1966, when global population growth rates were reaching an historic annual high of 2.1%, the United Nations began to include population technical assistance in its international development aid programs. Population assistance grew rapidly over the next half-dozen years, with the United States, other developed countries, and international organizations such as the World Bank, all beginning to contribute funds. With passage of the Foreign Assistance Act of 1961, Congress first authorized research on international family planning and population issues and, in 1965, the U.S. Agency for International Development (USAID) launched a series of population and reproductive health programs. In 1968, Congress specifically funded family planning aid activities and USAID began to purchase contraceptives for distribution through its programs in the developing world.

The first International Population Conference was held in 1974, followed by the second in Mexico City in 1984, and the third in Cairo in 1994.[1] The attention and funding given to international family planning programs are credited with helping to decrease population growth in developing countries from about a 1.7% per year average between 1980 and 2002, to a projected annual average of 1.2% between 2002 and 2015. Fertility rates have fallen in developing nations from 4.1 children per woman in 1980 to 3.0 in 2005 (if China is excluded from this calculation, however, the decline in fertility rates is less dramatic at 3.5 children in 2005). Nevertheless, while global population growth has slowed, the world's population reached 6 billion in 1999, 6.5 billion in 2005, and is expected to rise to 9.3 billion by 2050, with most of the growth occurring in developing nations. In 1960, 70% of the world's population lived in developing countries, and in 2005 the level had grown to 81%. These countries now account for 99% of world-wide population growth.[2]

The Population Statistics Debate

Population statistics alone are only part of a larger story. For the past thirty years and more, countries have heatedly debated what the statistics mean. Proponents of active family planning programs have held that high fertility rates and rapid population growth are serious impediments to a country's development. According to this school of thought, people are consumers, and no poor country can increase its standard of living and raise its per capita income while wrestling with the problems of trying to feed and care for a rapidly expanding population. Thus, poor and developing countries should invest in family planning programs as part of their economic development process.

On the opposing side, critics of active population planning programs hold that there is little or no correlation between rapid population growth and a country's economic development. Some argue that increased numbers of people provide added productive capacity; therefore, they say, high population growth rates actually can contribute to a country's ability to increase its standard of living. Proponents of this view argue that, at the very least, current economies of scale and global trading patterns have too many empirical variables and uncertainties to establish a direct correlation between population growth and economic development.

Evolution of U.S. Policy (1974-1994)

As the population debate evolved, many countries, including the United States, changed their views. At the 1974 international population conference, the United States and other donor countries asserted that high fertility rates were an impediment to economic development — a point that was then rejected by developing countries. In keeping with this view, in 1977 the Carter Administration proposed legislative language, later enacted in Sec. 104(d) of the Foreign Assistance Act of 1961, that sought to link population growth and traditional development assistance programs on the grounds that a high population growth rate could have a negative effect on other development objectives.

A decade later, at the second International Conference on Population in Mexico City in 1984, some participants reversed their positions. Many developing countries had become convinced of the urgent need to manage population growth, while U.S. officials asserted that population growth was not necessarily a negative force in economic development, but was instead a "neutral phenomenon." At Mexico City, Reagan Administration officials emphasized the need for developing countries to adopt sound economic policies that stressed open markets and an active private sector.

Nearly a decade later, the Clinton Administration changed the U.S. position on family planning programs by lifting restrictive U.S. provisions announced at the Mexico City Conference. At the 1994 International Conference on Population and Development in Cairo, U.S. officials emphasized support for family planning and reproductive health services, improving the status of women, and providing safe access to abortion.

Trends in Population Research

Since the 1994 Cairo conference, groups supporting strategies to limit rapid population growth have supported a broader agenda of initiatives that include the promotion of gender equality, increasing adolescent education on sexuality and reproductive health, and ensuring the universal right of health care, including reproductive health. Although endorsed at the July 1999 U.N. meeting of 179 nations to assess progress of the Cairo population conference recommendations, the issues of child education and government responsibilities for ensuring access to safe abortions in countries where the practice is legal were particularly controversial. Some governments opposed the broadening of the Cairo mandate and some, including Argentina, Nicaragua, and the Vatican, filed reservations to the recommendations reached by consensus.

More recently, new research suggests that there has been a significant decline in birthrates in several of the largest developing nations, including India, Brazil, and Egypt.[3] Some demographers conclude that global population projections for this century may need to be reduced by as much as one billion people. A U.N. report dated December 9, 2003 — "World Population 2300" — projects as a "medium scenario" that world population will peak in 2075 at 9.2 billion and then, as fertility rates in all countries reach below replacement levels, decline over the next 100 years to 8.3 billion. The report projects that if fertility rates return to replacement levels, world population would begin to rise, reaching 9 billion by 2300; otherwise, the number of people would remain at around 8.3 billion.

Although there are differences of opinion as to why fertility rates are falling —and whether the trend is universal throughout the developing world — a few demographers argue that the change has less to do with government family planning policies and foreign aid, and more to do with expanded women's rights in these countries. Women are choosing to have fewer children, they argue. Others also contend that with improved health conditions and lowered infant mortality rates, parents are deciding to have fewer babies because they are more confident that their children will survive.

Policy and Funding Issues in the U.S. Family Planning Debate

Throughout the debate on family planning — at times the most contentious foreign aid issue considered by Congress — the cornerstone of U.S. policy has remained a commitment to international family planning programs based on principles of volunteerism and informed choice that give participants access to information on all major methods of birth control. At present, USAID maintains family planning projects in more than 60 countries that include counseling and services, training of health workers, contraceptive supplies and distribution, financial management, public education and marketing, and biomedical and contraceptive research and development. USAID applies a broad reproductive health approach to its family planning programs, increasingly integrating it with other interventions regarding maternal and child health, the enhancement of the status of women, and HIV prevention.

In addition to differences of opinion over how population growth affects economic development in developing countries, family planning assistance has become a source of substantial controversy among U.S. policymakers on two other issues: 1) the use of federal funds to perform or promote abortions abroad and how to deal with evidence of coercion in some foreign national family planning programs, especially in China; and 2) setting appropriate and effective funding levels for family planning assistance.

Abortion and Coercion

The bitterest controversies in U.S. family planning policy have erupted over abortion — in particular, the degree to which abortions and coercive programs occur in other countries' family planning programs, the extent to which U.S. funds should be granted to or withheld from such countries and organizations that administer these programs, and the effect that withholding U.S. funds will have on global population growth and family planning services in developing nations. These issues essentially stem from the contentious domestic debate over U.S. abortion policy that has continued since the Supreme Court's 1973 *Roe v. Wade* decision holding that the Constitution protects a woman's decision whether to terminate her pregnancy. In every Congress since 1973, abortion opponents have introduced constitutional amendments or legislation that would prohibit abortions, but none has been enacted. As an alternative, abortion critics have persuaded Congress to attach numerous provisions to annual appropriation measures banning the use of federal funds for performing abortions.

Much of this debate has focused on domestic spending bills, especially restrictions on abortions under the Medicaid program in the Labor/Health and Human Services appropriation legislation. Nevertheless, the controversy spilled over into U.S. foreign aid policy almost immediately when Congress approved an amendment to the Foreign Assistance Act of 1961 in late 1973 (Section 104(f)). The act prohibits the use of foreign development assistance to 1) pay for the performance of abortions or involuntary sterilizations, 2) to motivate or coerce any person to practice abortions, or 3) to coerce or provide persons with any financial incentive to undergo sterilizations. Since 1981, Congress has enacted nearly identical restrictions in annual Foreign Operations appropriation bills.

For the past 25 years, both congressional actions and administration directives have restricted U.S. population assistance in various ways, including those set out in the Foreign Assistance Act of 1961, and more recent executive regulations and appropriation provisions prohibiting *indirect* support for coercive family planning (specifically in China) and abortion activities related to the work of international and foreign NGOs. Two issues in particular which were initiated in 1984 — the Mexico City policy involving funding for foreign non-governmental organizations, and restrictions on funding for the U.N. Population Fund (UNFPA) because of its activities in China — have remained controversial and continue as prominent features in the population assistance debate.

The Mexico City Policy[4]

In 1984, the Reagan Administration announced that it would further restrict U.S. population aid by terminating USAID support for any foreign organizations (but not national governments) that were involved in voluntary abortion activities, even if such activities were undertaken with non-U.S. funds. U.S. officials presented the revised policy at the 2nd U.N. International Conference on Population in Mexico City in 1984. Thereafter, it become known as the "Mexico City policy." During the George H.W. Bush Administration, efforts were made in Congress to overturn the Mexico City policy and rely on existing congressional restrictions in the Foreign Assistance Act of 1961 banning direct U.S. funding of abortions and coerced sterilizations. Provisions adopted by the House and/or Senate that would have reversed the policy, however, were removed from legislation under threat of a presidential veto.

Critics charge, however, that the Mexico City policy is a violation of free speech and the rights of women to choose. They contend that the policy undermines maternal health care services offered in developing nations and may actually contribute to the rise in the number of abortions performed, including some that are unsafe and illegal. They further emphasize that family planning organizations may cut back on services because they are unsure of the full implications of the restrictions and do not want to risk losing eligibility for USAID funding. Opponents also believe that the conditions of the Mexico City policy undermine relations between the U.S. government and foreign NGOs and multilateral groups, creating a situation in which the United States challenges their right to determine how to spend their own money and imposes a so-called gag order on their ability to promote changes to abortion laws and regulations in developing nations. The latter, these critics note, would be unconstitutional if applied to American groups working in the United States.

Mexico City Policy Removed

President Clinton, in a January 22, 1993 memo to USAID, lifted restrictions imposed by the Reagan and Bush Administrations on grants to family planning NGOs — in effect ending the Mexico City policy. The memo noted that the policy had extended beyond restrictions in the Foreign Assistance Act and was not mandated by law. In his remarks, President Clinton explained that this step would "reverse a policy that has seriously undermined much needed efforts to promote safe and effective family planning programs abroad, and will allow us to once again provide leadership in helping to stabilize world population."[5]

Past Efforts to Legislate the Mexico City Policy

Beginning in 1993, abortion opponents in Congress attempted to legislate modified terms of the Mexico City policy. Under threat of a Presidential veto and resistance from the Senate, Mexico City restrictions had not been enacted into law until the November 1999 passage of the Consolidated Appropriations Act for FY2000 (P.L. 106-113). The White House accepted the family planning conditions in exchange for congressional support of the payment of nearly $1 billion owed by the United States to the United Nations. The restrictions expired at the end of FY2000.

Under terms of Section 599D of P.L. 106-113, the President could waive the certification requirement for up to $15 million in grants to groups that would otherwise be ineligible. President Clinton exercised the waiver and further instructed USAID to implement Section 599D in a way that would minimize the impact on U.S. funded family planning programs. Nine organizations refused to certify under the terms of P.L. 106-113, including two of the largest recipients of USAID population aid grants — IPPF and the World Health Organization (WHO). These nine non-certifying organizations received about $8.4 million in FY2000 grants, of which IPPF accounted for $5 million and WHO roughly $2.5 million. These conditions, enacted in an appropriation act, expired at the end of FY2000.

Bush Administration Restores the Mexico City Policy

On January 22, 2001, President George W. Bush revoked the Clinton Administration memorandum and restored in full the terms of the Mexico City restrictions. In making the announcement, however, the White House Press Secretary stated that the "President is committed to maintaining the $425 million funding level provided in the FY2001 appropriation because he knows that one of the best ways to prevent abortion is by providing quality voluntary family planning services."[6]

As was the case during the 1980s and early 1990s when the Mexico City policy was in place, foreign NGOs and international organizations, as a condition for receipt of U.S. funds, would need to certify that they would not perform or actively promote abortions as a method of family planning in other countries. President Bush, in announcing the policy change, noted that American taxpayer funds should not be used to pay for abortions or to advocate or actively promote abortion. Supporters of the certification requirement argue that even though permanent law bans USAID funds from being used to perform or promote abortions, money is fungible; organizations receiving American-taxpayer funding can use USAID resources for legal activities while diverting money raised from other sources to perform abortions or lobby to change abortion laws and regulations. The certification process, they contend, stops the fungibility "loophole."

Bush Administration Mexico City Policy Guidelines

On February 15, 2001, USAID released specific contract clauses necessary to implement the President's directive. The guidelines state that U.S. NGOs receiving USAID grants cannot furnish assistance to foreign NGOs that 1) perform or actively promote abortion as a method of family planning in USAID-recipient countries; or 2) furnish assistance to other foreign NGOs that conduct such activities. When USAID provides assistance directly to a foreign NGO, the organization must certify that it does not now or will not during the term of the grant perform or actively promote abortion as a method of family planning in USAID-recipient countries or provide financial support to other foreign NGOs that carry out such activities. The implementing regulations contain several exceptions, including the following:

- Abortions may be performed if the life of the mother would be endangered if the fetus were carried to term or following rape or incest; health care facilities may treat injuries or illnesses caused by legal or illegal abortions (post-abortion care).
- "Passive" responses by family planning counselors to questions about abortion from pregnant women who have already decided to have a legal abortion are not considered an act of promoting abortion; referrals for abortion as a result of rape, incest, or where the mother's life would be endangered, or for post-abortion care are permitted.

USAID is able to continue support foreign governments, either directly or through a grantee, even in cases where the government includes abortion in its family planning program. Money provided to such governments, however, must be placed in a segregated account and none of the funds may be drawn to finance abortion activities.

The President issued a memorandum on August 29, 2003, for the Secretary of State, directing that the Mexico City policy conditions be applied to State Department programs in the same way they are applied to USAID activities. This directive mostly impacts State

Department-managed refugee programs, large portions of which are implemented by international organizations and NGOs. The President's memorandum, however, stated that the policy would not apply to multilateral organizations that are associations of governments, presumably referring to the U.N. High Commissioner for Refugees, among others. The President further stated that the Mexico City policy would not apply to foreign aid funds authorized under P.L. 108-25, the United States Leadership Against HIV/AIDS, Tuberculosis, and Malaria Act of 2003.

Related Mexico City Policy Issues

The Bush Administration policy to prevent foreign assistance from supporting organizations performing or promoting abortions has also shaped other U.S. policy positions at multilateral fora. In October 2004, international family planning activists sought to commemorate the 10 year anniversary of the Cairo International Conference on Population and Development (ICPD) with a statement endorsing the 1994 recommendations. Although more than 250 global leaders, including 85 current and 22 former heads of state and government from Europe, Asia, and Africa, signed the document, President Bush chose not to add his signature. According to State Department officials, while the United States supports the goals and objectives of the Cairo conference, the U.S. could not join others in signing the "world leaders" statement because it included the concept of "sexual rights." This term, these officials said, does not have a consensus definition and was not part of the ICPD platform. Critics, however, note that at the 1995 Beijing women's conference, "sexual rights" was included in the adopted action plan and supported by United States.

Restrictions on United Nations Population Fund (UNFPA) Funding[7]

At the 1984 Mexico City Conference, the Reagan Administration instituted a new policy relating to UNFPA.[8] The Administration required that UNFPA provide "concrete assurances that [it] is not engaged in, or does not provide funding for, abortion or coercive family planning programs." It was was particularly concerned with UNFPA's activities in China, where there is evidence of coercive family planning practices.

Subsequently, Congress legislated a more restrictive UNFPA policy — aimed at coercive Chinese family planning programs and UNFPA's continuing operations in the country — by enacting the "Kemp-Kasten amendment" in the FY1985 Supplemental Appropriations Act (P.L. 99-88). This language prohibited the use of appropriated funds for any organization or program, as determined by the President, found to be supporting or participating "in the management" of a program of coercive abortion or involuntary sterilization. Following enactment of P.L. 99-88, USAID announced that $10 million of $46 million that had been directed for UNFPA during FY1985 would be redirected to other programs, and later said that the United States would not contribute to UNFPA at all in 1986. Most of the $25 million that was originally allocated for UNFPA was spent for other international family planning activities. Even though this pattern to redirect UNFPA transfers to other population assistance programs continued, critics of the Kemp-Kasten amendment and the President's determination to suspend contributions asserted that UNFPA was the world's most effective family planning organization, and that the quality of services provided in developing nations outside of China suffered due to the unwillingness of the United States to support them. At the time of suspension, U.S. payments represented nearly one-third of UNFPA's annual budget. From 1986 through 1993, no U.S. contributions went to UNFPA.

The Clinton Administration lifted the ban on UNFPA contributions, making available $14.5 million in FY1993 but stipulating that funds could not be used in China. Again, congressional critics of China's family planning practices attempted unsuccessfully to attach provisions to various foreign aid bills banning U.S. contributions unless UNFPA withdrew from China or the President could certify that China no longer maintained a coercive family planning program. While the United States continued to support UNFPA during the next eight years (except for FY1999), Congress attached restrictions in appropriation measures that in most cases reduced the U.S. contribution by the proportionate share of UNFPA funds spent on China.

Bush Administration and UNFPA

For FY2002, Congress provided "not more than" $34 million for UNFPA. But in mid-January 2002, the Bush Administration placed a hold on U.S. contributions to UNFPA, pending a review of the organization's program in China. The White House said it initiated the review because of new evidence that coercive practices continued in counties where UNFPA concentrated its programs.[9]

Since the July 2002 determination, the Administration has transferred $34 million from each of FY2002, FY2004, and FY2005 appropriations, and $25 million from FY2003 funds that would have otherwise been provided to UNFPA to support bilateral family planning programs and activities combating human trafficking and prostitution. Approximately $22.5 million in unused UNFPA funds from FY2006 was be transferred to the International Organizations and Program (IOP) account. On September 6, 2007, the Administration sent a letter to Members of Congress stating that UNFPA is ineligible for FY2007 funds because of its support of coercive family planning practices in China.[10] Unused FY2007 IOP funds designated for UNFPA will likely be transferred to other family planning programs.

State Department Team Assesses UNFPA Program in China

While most observers agree that coercive family planning practices continue in China, differences remain over the extent, if any, to which UNFPA is involved in involuntary activities and whether UNFPA should operate at all in a country where such conditions exist. Given conflicting reports, a State Department investigative team visited China in May 2002 and reported a series of findings and recommendations. The team found no evidence that UNFPA "has knowingly supported or participated in the management of a program of coercive abortion or involuntary sterilization" in China, and recommended the United States release not more than $34 million of previously appropriated funds to UNFPA.[11]

Nevertheless, on July 22, 2002, Secretary of State Powell, to whom the President had delegated the decision, announced that UNFPA was in violation of Kemp-Kasten and ineligible for U.S. funding. The State Department's analysis of the Secretary's determination found that even though UNFPA did not "knowingly" support or participate in a coercive practice, that alone would not preclude the application of Kemp-Kasten.[12] Instead, a finding that the recipient of U.S. funds —in this case UNFPA — simply supports or participates in such a program, whether knowingly or unknowingly, would trigger the restriction. The assessment team found that the Chinese government imposed fines and penalties on families ("social compensation fees") that have children exceeding the number approved by the government. The Department further noted that UNFPA had funded computers and data-processing equipment that had helped strengthen the management of the

Chinese State Family Planning Commission. Beyond the legitimate uses of these and other items financed by UNFPA, such equipment facilitated, in the view of the State Department, China's ability to impose social compensation fees or perform coercive abortions. The State Department analysis concluded that UNFPA's involvement in China's family planning program, "allows the Chinese government to implement more effectively its program of coercive abortion."

On September 17, 2005, the State Department stated that the United States had been urging UNFPA and China to modify the organization's program in a manner that would permit U.S. support to resume, but that no key changes had occurred that would allow a resumption of U.S. funding under the conditions of the Kemp-Kasten provision. Subsequently, on October 18, USAID notified Congress that the reprogrammed UNFPA set-aside would be made available to expand family planning and reproductive health programs in 14 other countries.[13]

U.S. Response to the New UNFPA China Program

The September 17 announcement followed a June 22, 2005 UNFPA Executive Board meeting to consider UNFPA's new five-year, $27 million program for China. At the meeting, Kelly Ryan, Deputy Assistant Secretary of State for the Bureau of Population, Refugees and Migration, argued that UNFPA should end its operations in China because of the coercive nature of China's family planning programs. Two days later, State Department spokesperson, Sean McCormick, issued a statement saying the United States was "disappointed" that UNFPA had decided to continue financial and technical support to the Chinese birth limitation program. He noted that U.S. opposition was not aimed at UNFPA but was a "matter of principle," based on strong American opposition to "human rights abuses associated with coercive birth limitation regimes." He acknowledged that UNFPA does not approve of coercive policies but that the organization's continued presence in China offered a "seal of approval" for Chinese policies.

Opposition to the State Department Determination

Critics of the Administration's decision opposed it for a number of reasons, including the loss of $34 million, an amount that represented about 9% of UNFPA income in 2001. They argued that access to voluntary family planning programs by persons in around 140 countries would be reduced, undermining the health of women and children, increasing unwanted pregnancies, and increasing the likelihood of higher numbers of abortions. Still other critics were concerned about the possible application of the Administration's interpretation of Kemp-Kasten for other international organizations operating in China and to which the U.S. contributes — for example, UNICEF, WHO, and the U.N. Development Program.

Other Related State Department Determinations

There have been several other State Department determinations related to the July 2002 decision regarding UNFPA. On August 6, 2003, for example, the State Department decided that it would fund a $1 million HIV/AIDS program supporting African and Asian refugees only if the implementing NGO group — Reproductive Health for Refugees Consortium — did not include Marie Stopes International among its members. Marie Stopes International is a British-based reproductive health organization that at the time was a major implementing partner of UNFPA in China. The State Department, while not making a legal determination under the Kemp-Kasten amendment, felt that an action not to fund Marie Stopes International would be an "approach most consistent with U.S. policy." On August 11, however, the Consortium declined to accept the $1 million grant due to the exclusion of Marie Stopes International.

In another decision, the Administration notified the Global Health Council in April 2004 that the U.S. government would not provide funding for the Council's 31st annual meeting in June 2004 because UNFPA would be a participant. Reportedly, U.S. officials told representatives of international organizations and NGOs that UNICEF, WHO, and other organizations that continued involvement in joint programs with UNFPA might jeopardize their funding support from the United States.[14]

Family Planning Conditions in China

As noted, much of this debate has focused on UNFPA's programs in China, both because of China's well-known population growth problem and because of widespread publicity given to reports of coercion in its family planning programs. China's population increased from 500 million in 1950 to 1.008 billion according to the 1982 census — an average annual growth rate of 2%, or a doubling of the population every 36 years. (Although the 2% rate is not particularly large by developing country standards, many consider a lower rate crucial to China's economic development prospects given the country's already huge population size.)

Chinese authorities came to view control of population growth not simply as an important priority, but as a necessity for the nation's survival. In an attempt to reach a 1% annual population growth rate, Chinese authorities, in 1979, instituted a policy of allowing only one child per couple, providing monetary bonuses and other benefits as incentives to comply. Women with one living child who became pregnant a second time were said to be subjected to rigorous pressure to end the pregnancy and undergo sterilization; couples who actually had a second child faced heavy fines, employment demotions, and other penalties. Chinese leaders have admitted that coerced abortions and involuntary sterilizations occur, but insist that those involved are acting outside the law and are punished, particularly through the Administrative Procedure Law enacted in October 1990. Chinese authorities have termed female infanticide an "intolerable crime" that must be punished by law.

Other press reports suggest that the Chinese State Family Planning Commission (SFPC) has softened some of its previous harsh tactics to limit population growth. A number of counties have ended the system of permits for pregnancy and quotas for the number of children that can be born annually. When it launched in January 1998 a new $20 million, five-year program in China, UNFPA announced that SFPC officials had agreed to drop birth targets in the 32 counties where U.N. activities would be focused. And in May 1999, the city of Beijing ended an eight-year policy that women had to be at least 24 years old to bear a child and lifted the requirement for couples to obtain a certificate before having a child.

On September 1, 2002, China adopted the Population and Family Planning Law, the country's first formal law on this subject. The law, which requires couples who have an unapproved child to pay a "social compensation fee" and extends preferential treatment to couples who abide by the birth limits, is intended to standardize the implementation of the Government's birth limitation policies. The State Department Country Reports on Human Rights Practices for 2006 (dated March 2007), however, found that enforcement of the law varied by location.

The broad question concerning the degree of coercive family planning practices in China remains a controversial matter. The State Department's human rights report concluded that "Central Government policy formally prohibits the use of physical coercion to compel persons to submit to abortion or sterilization. Because it is illegal, the use of physical coercion was difficult to document. A few cases were reported during the year [2004]... However, the Government does not consider social compensation fees and other administrative punishments to be coercive."[15] Chinese officials acknowledge past instances of forced abortion and involuntary sterilizations, but say this is no longer the case and characterize the social compensation fees as not coercive, but a "disincentive" or "necessary form of economic restraint."[16]

Recent attention has focused on reports documenting a campaign by local family planning officials around the city of Linyi in Shandong Province to force couples with two children to undergo sterilizations or to demand women pregnant with a third child have an abortion. Local activists are pursuing a class-action lawsuit against the government. The group's leader, Chen Guangcheng, was placed under house arrest and subsequently sentenced to four years and three months in prison.[17] In mid-September 2005, China's National Population and Family Planning Commission acknowledged that illegal coercive practices had occurred, and that responsible officials had been dismissed and that some had been detained.[18]

Following the May 2002 State Department investigation of Chinese policies, senior Department officials began a series of discussions with China regarding its birth planning law. Arthur Dewey, Assistant Secretary of State for Population, Refugees, and Migration, told the House International Relations Committee on December 14, 2004, that in six rounds of talks with Chinese officials, there had been "encouraging movement" in China's approach to population policy and the reduction of coercive practices.[19] Nevertheless, Assistant Secretary Dewey said that the social compensation fee policy set out in China's national law on Population and Birth Planning is a "harsh and effective enforcement tool" that is used to force women to have an abortion, and is therefore regarded as a coercive policy. While negotiations have resulted in some progress, he concluded that China's policies have not been altered enough to allow the Bush Administration to resume UNFPA funding.

As noted previously, U.S. officials continued to voice their opposition at a UNFPA executive board meeting on June 22, 2005, where members met to consider a new, five-year (2006-2010), $27 million UNFPA program in China. A State Department press release on June 24 again acknowledged that China had made some progress in its approach to population issues, but argued that Beijing's birth limitation policy continues to contain several coercive elements, including the social maintenance fee for unplanned births, and regulations that limit choices by women other than to undergo an abortion. At the June 22 meeting, China's deputy U.N. ambassador Zhang Yishan argued that due to the size of China's population, it had to maintain a strong family planning program, and that without the policies of the last 30 years, China's population would have grown by 300 million additional people. He countered that, by law, family planning workers are not permitted to utilize coercive measures in their work.

The UNFPA Executive Board approved the new five-year program for China on January 30, 2006. Prior to the signing, U.S. Deputy Representative to the United Nations, Ambassador Alejandro Wolff, expressed disappointment that no substantive changes had been made to the draft plan that had been reviewed in mid-2005. He argued that UNFPA assistance provided a "de facto United Nations 'seal of approval'" to Chinese "abhorrent" practices. He further asserted that the new Country Program Document for China was incorrect in its claim that China was committed to implementing the Cairo Population Conference action plan, a program that excluded coercive practices in family planning activities.[20] A group of ten European nations disagreed, however, issuing a statement saying that China did conform to the program of 1994 International Conference on Population and Development.[21]

Funding Levels

Since 1965, USAID has obligated over $6.6 billion in assistance for international population planning. In many years, and especially over the past decade, the appropriate level of funding for population assistance has been controversial, and at times, linked directly with differences concerning Mexico City restrictions and abortion. Until FY1996, Congress generally supported higher funding levels for population aid than proposed by the President, especially during the Reagan and Bush Administrations. Appropriations peaked in FY1995 at $577 million.

During the balance of the Clinton Administration, however, Congress cut and placed restrictions on bilateral funding. Amounts for bilateral programs fell to $356 million in FY1996, but grew steadily to $425 million by FY2001. When President Bush took office in January 2001, the White House said that it would maintain the $425 million funding level of the previous Administration. While budgets submitted by President Bush adhered to the $425 million target through FY2006, in every year Congress increased funding levels, as shown in table 1. Bilateral funds reached their highest totals since the mid-1990s in FY2002 and FY2003 at $446.5 million, but fell back somewhat more recently. In some years beginning in FY2002, bilateral family planning levels have received additional resources when UNFPA-earmarked funds were reprogrammed for bilateral activities after UNFPA was determined to be ineligible for U.S. support.

Financing family planning and basic reproductive health care programs in developing countries became a major issue at the 1994 Cairo population conference. Participating nations agreed that foreign aid donors would provide one-third, or $5.7 billion, of the annual costs of such services that were estimated to grow to about $17 billion in 2000. A July 1999 conference assessing implementation of the 1994 Cairo strategy, however, found that industrialized countries had fallen far short of the financing goal, providing only about $1.9 billion per year. It also noted that donor allocations still fall far below the targets set at Cairo.[22] A more recent analysis suggests a different trend, noting that donor nations contributed $2.3 billion in 2002, the largest amount ever. Similarly, the UNFPA announced in January 2007 that the number of donors to its program had increased from 166 in 2004 to 180 in 2006. The amount promised from donors reached a record of $360 million in 2006.[23]

Table 1. U.S. Population Assistance, FY1994-2007 (appropriations of millions of $)

	1994	1995	1996	1997	1998	1999	2000	2001	2002[c]	2003[c]	2004[c]	2005[c]	2006[c]	2007[e]
Bilateral Aid	485.1	541.6	356.0	385.0	385.0	385.0	372.5[a]	425.0	465.5	443.5	429.5	448.1	440.0[d]	357.0
UNFPA	40.0	35.0	22.8	25.0	20.0	0.0	21.5[b]	21.5[b]	0.0	0.0	0.0	0.0	0.0	
Total	525.1	576.6	378.8	410.0	405.0	385.0	394.0	446.5	465.5	443.5	429.5	448.1	440.0[d]	

Source: USAID/Office of Population and CRS calculations. Amounts are adjusted for rescissions in selected years.

a. The bilateral FY2000 aid level reflects a transfer of $12.5 million from population assistance to child survival activities. b. UNFPA amounts for FY2000 and FY2001 reflect a $3.5 million deduction due to legislative restrictions. c. In each of FY2002-FY2006, the Administration determined that UNFPA was ineligible for U.S. funding because of its programs in China, and withheld appropriated funds. The withheld funds were reallocated for USAID bilateral family planning, vulnerable children, and counter-trafficking in persons programs. d. $440 million is the amount appropriated for bilateral aid per P.L. 109-102. Figure does not include 1% rescission required by P.L. 109-148. e. Any UNFPA contribution for FY2007 is included in the Administration's bilateral family planning request of $357 million. Foreign Operations programs are currently operating under a continuing resolution, and the final bilateral aid for FY2007 has not yet been determined.

International Family Planning Legislation

FY2007 and FY2008 Foreign Operations Appropriations

Administration Request, FY2008

The Administration's FY2008 request for bilateral international family planning and reproductive health activities totals $324.8 million.[24] This represents a $32.2 million decrease from the FY2007 Administration request of $357 million, and a $115.2 million decrease from the enacted 2006 funding level of $440 million. The Administration cites "significant successes that have been achieved after 40 years of worldwide family planning efforts" as justification for decreased funding. It proposed that $25 million of the $324.8 million bilateral family planning request be made available for UNFPA if the organization becomes eligible under the terms of the Kemp-Kasten amendment.

House and Senate Appropriations, FY2008

On June 21, 2007, the House of Representatives passed H.R. 2764, the State, Foreign Operations, and Related Programs Appropriations Bill, FY2008, that appropriates $441 million for reproductive health and voluntary family planning programs ($116.2 above the President's request). The Committee on Appropriations report accompanying the bill, H.Rept. 110-197, directs that no less that $375 million should come from Child Survival and Health funds and that $66 million should come from other accounts. It also directs that $40 million be made available to UNFPA if it becomes eligible for U.S. support under the terms of the Kemp-Kasten amendment. It specifies that $23 million of the $40 million should be derived from the International Organizations and Programs (IOP) account.

The House-passed version of H.R. 2764 also adds a reporting requirement to the Kemp-Kasten amendment. Section 660 specifies that any determination made under the authority of the amendment "must be made no later than six months after the date of enactment of this Act, and must be accompanied by a comprehensive analysis as well as the complete evidence and criteria used to make the determination." The bill requires the Secretary of State to submit a report on UNFPA funding to the appropriate congressional committees no later than four months after the bill is enacted. The report shall indicate "the amount of funds that the UNFPA is budgeting for the year in which the report is submitted for a country program in the People's Republic of China."[25] Under the provision, if the Secretary of State's report indicates that UNFPA funds will be used for a program in China, then the funds "shall be deducted from the funds made available to the UNFPA after March 1 for obligation for the remainder of the fiscal year in which the report is submitted."[26]

The Senate passed its version of H.R. 2764 on September 6, 2007.[27] The bill appropriates $461.06 million for family planning and reproductive health programs (the House appropriated $441 million).[28] It does not designate a specific dollar amount for UNFPA. Unlike the House-passed bill, it does not add reporting requirements to the Kemp-Kasten amendment. During floor debate for H.R. 2764, Senator Barbara Boxer proposed an amendment that many contend could overturn the Mexico City Policy.[29] The amendment, which was adopted by a vote of 53-41, states:

> Notwithstanding any other provision of law, regulation, or policy, in determining eligibility for assistance authorized under part I of the Foreign Assistance Act of 1961 (22

> U.S.C. 2151 et. seq.), foreign nongovernmental organizations shall not be ineligible for such assistance solely on the basis of health or medical services, including counseling and referral services, provided by such organizations with non-United States Government funds if such services do not violate the laws of the country in which they are being provided and would not violated United States Federal Law if provided in the United States, and shall not be subject to requirements relating to the use of non-United States Government funds for advocacy and lobbying activities other than those that apply to United States non governmental organizations receiving assistance under part I of such Act.[30]

Contraceptive Distribution Provision

Both the FY2008 House and Senate-passed State Foreign Operations appropriations bills continue previous restrictions on the use of family planning funds but allow for the provision of contraceptives by non-governmental organizations that would not otherwise be eligible for family planning funds because of the Mexico City policy.[31] Section 622 of both bills states:

> ...no contract or grant for the exclusive purpose of providing donated contraceptives in developing countries shall be denied to any nongovernmental organization solely on the basis of the policy contained in the President's March 28, 2001, Memorandum to the Administrator of USAID with respect to providing contraceptives in developing countries, or any comparable administration policy regarding the provision of contraceptives.

Supporters of the provision maintain that providing contraceptives to NGOs that might otherwise not receive U.S. assistance will ultimately reduce abortion rates. They emphasize that the amendment does not undermine the Mexico City policy because it only provides contraceptives, and not funding, to these organizations. Opponents of the provision argue that money is fungible, and therefore any funds the organizations saves from U.S. contraceptive donations can be redirected to activities that promote and perform abortion as a method of family planning.[32] Such contributions, opponents argue, violate the intent of the Mexico City policy.

FY2007

The President's FY2007 request of $357 million marked the first time that the Bush Administration sought less than $425 million for international family planning activities. If UNFPA becomes eligible for U.S. support, a U.S. contribution of $25 million could be drawn from the $357 million request. This is the second year that the Administration proposed that $25 million for UNFPA be drawn from its total family planning request rather than in addition to amounts requested for bilateral programs. It is also the second year that the Administration did not set aside a $25 million reserve in the IOP account.[33]

The House Foreign Operations Appropriations Subcommittee reported H.R. 5522, the FY2007 Foreign Operations Appropriations bill, on May 15, 2006. The Committee recommended a total of $432 million for reproductive health and family planning activities, an increase of some $75 million over the Administration request. Of the total, $350 million would come from the Child Survival and Health Programs fund. If the UNFPA becomes eligible for U.S. support, $34 million would be available, of which $22.3 million would be drawn from the International Organizations and Programs (IOP) account, and $11.7 million from Child Survival and Health. In September 2007, the Administration determined that

UNFPA is ineligible for FY2007 funds because of its support for coercive family planning practices in China.[34] Unused IOP funds meant for UNFPA will likely be transferred to other family planning programs.

Currently, foreign operations programs are being funded under the terms of a continuing resolution (H.R. 5631/P.L. 109-289, as amended), which provides funding similar to the FY2006 level with some adjustments. Thus, the current level of funding for bilateral family planning activities should be around $440 million — the enacted level for bilateral population assistance activities in FY2006 (see H.R. 3057/P.L. 109-102).

Other International Family Planning Legislation (110th Congress)

H.R. 619 prohibits the application of certain restrictive eligibility requirements on foreign NGOs that provide development and humanitarian assistance. It was introduced on January 22, 2007, by Representative Nita Lowey, and was referred to the Committee on Foreign Affairs.

H.R. 1095, the Taxpayers' Freedom of Conscience Act of 2007, states that no federal official may expend any federal funds for any population control or population planning program or any family planning activities (including any abortion procedure), regardless of whether the program or activity is foreign or domestic. The bill was introduced by Representative Ron Paul on February 15, 2007, and was referred to the Committees on Foreign Affairs and Energy and Commerce.

H.R. 1225, the Focus on Family Health Worldwide Act of 2007, seeks to amend the Foreign Assistance Act of 1961 to improve voluntary family planning programs in developing countries. Activities supported by the bill include improving public awareness of voluntary family planning programs and expanding training for heath care providers. The bill was introduced on February 28, 2007, by Representative Betty McCollum and referred to the Committee on Foreign Affairs.

H.R. 2114, the Repairing Young Women's Lives Around the World Act, provides "a United States voluntary contribution to the United Nations Population Fund only for the prevention, treatment, and repair of obstetric fistula." The bill was introduced on May 2, 2007, by Representative Carolyn Maloney and was referred to the Committee on Foreign Affairs.

H.R. 2367, the Ensuring Access to Contraceptives Act of 2007, amends the Foreign Assistance Act of 1961 to "authorize assistance to provide contraceptives in developing countries in order to prevent unintended pregnancies, abortions, and the transmission of sexually transmitted infections, including HIV/AIDS." It was introduced on May 17, 2007, by Representative Russ Carnahan and was referred to the Committee on Foreign Affairs.

H.R. 2604, the United Nations Population Fund Women's Health and Dignity Act, provides financial and other support to UNFPA to "carry out activities to save women's lives, limit the incidence of abortion and maternal mortality associated with unsafe abortion ...[and] promote access to safe and reliable family planning." It was introduced on June 7, 2007, by Representative Joseph Crowley and was referred to the Committee on Foreign Affairs.

REFERENCES

[1] The conferences were coordinated by the United Nations. More information is available at [http://www.un.org/esa/devagenda/population.html].

[2] Population Reference Bureau, Frequently Asked Questions About the PRB World Population Data Sheet, (2005).

[3] See, for example, "Population Estimates Fall as Poor Women Assert Control," *New York Times*, March 10, 2002.

[4] For a more detailed discussion of the original Mexico City policy, its implementation, and impact, see CRS Report RL30830, *International Family Planning: The "Mexico City" Policy*, by Larry Nowels.

[5] President Bill Clinton, "Remarks on Signing Memorandums on Medical Research and Reproductive Health and an Exchange With Reporters," January 22, 1993.

[6] The White House. Office of the Secretary. *Restoration of the Mexico City Policy,* January 22, 2001.

[7] For more detailed information regarding UNFPA, see CRS Report RL32703, *The U.N. Population Fund: Background and the U.S. Funding Debate*, by Luisa Blanchfield, Connie Veillette, and Larry Nowels.

[8] UNFPA is a U.N. specialized agency that "supports countries in using population data for policies and programs" to improve reproductive health, prevent HIV/AIDS, promote gender equality, and make motherhood safer. UNFPA was the lead U.N. agency for the 1994 International Conference on Population and Development in Cairo. For further information on UNFPA's mandate and activities, see [http://www.unfpa.org/].

[9] See House International Relations Committee hearing, Coercive Population Control in China: New Evidence of Forced Abortion and Forced Sterilization, October 17, 2001, and a Senate Foreign Relations Committee hearing, U.S. Funding for the U.N. Population Fund: The Effect on Women's Lives, February 27, 2002.

[10] "White House: No U.N. Funding for China," *The Associated Press,* September 7, 2007.

[11] See [http://www.state.gov/g/prm/rls/rpt/2002/12122.htm] for report's full text.

[12] See [http://www.state.gov/g/prm/rls/other/12128.htm] for a full text of the determination.

[13] The most significant increases were made in programs for Georgia, Madagascar, Romania, Russia, Rwanda, and Ukraine.

[14] Christopher Marquis, "U.S. Is Accused of Trying to Isolate U.N. Population Unit," *New York Times*, June 21, 2004.

[15] "Country Reports on Human Rights Practices, 2004 — China," U.S. Department of State, Bureau of Democracy, Human Rights and Labor, February 28, 2005, available at [http://www.state.gov/g/drl/rls/hrrpt/2004/41640.htm].

[16] U.S. Department of State, Assessment Team Report, May 29, 2002.

[17] For more information, see "Country Reports on Human Rights Practices, 2006 — China," U.S. Department of State, Bureau of Democracy, Human Rights and Labor, March 6, 2007, available at [http://www.state.gov/g/drl/rls/hrrpt/2006/78771.htm].

[18] Benjamin Kang Lim, "Blind China Activist Under House Arrest Since September," *Reuters*, January 6, 2006; Philip Pan, "Who Controls the Family? Blind Activist Leads Peasants in Legal Challenge to Abuses of China's Population Growth Policy,"

Washington Post, August 27, 2005; and "China Terse About Action on Abuses of One-Child Policy," *Washington Post*, September 20, 2005.

[19] Dewey cited, for example, the elimination of a requirement for married couples to obtain government permission prior to pregnancy in 25 of China's 31 provinces, municipalities, and autonomous regions. He also noted the government's launch of a public information project highlighting the status of the girl child. He viewed this as a positive step towards ending discrimination in China against girls and women.

[20] U.S. Mission to the United Nations. Ambassador Wolff: Remarks on Proposed UNFPA Sixth Country Program for China, January 26, 2006.

[21] UN Population Fund Endorses 27-million-dollar China Program. Agence France Presse, January 30, 2006.

[22] Population Action International, Progress and Promises: Trends in International Assistance for Reproductive Health and Population, 2004.

[23] "Record Number of Countries Contributed Record Amount to UNFPA in 2006," UNFPA Press Release, January 15, 2007.

[24] The Administration requests $301.7 million for family planning and reproductive health activities. It also requests $14.3 million in Economic Support Funds (ESF), $7.1 million for the FREEDOM Support Act (FSA), and $1.7 million for Eastern Europe and Baltic States Assistance (SEED) for family planning and reproductive health programs.

[25] Ibid. Sec. 660.

[26] The provision also states, "Nothing in this section shall be construed to limit the authority of the President to deny funds to any organization by reason of the application of another provision of this Act or any other provision of law." [Sec. 660(f) of H.R. 2764 as passed by the House of Representatives, June 21, 2007.]

[27] The Senate Committee on Appropriations reported H.R. 2764 on June 22, 2007. The bill, as marked up by the committee, attempted to modify the Kemp-Kasten amendment from previous years. It stated: "... none of the funds made available in this Act, nor any unobligated balances from prior appropriations may be made available to any organization or program which directly supports coercive abortion or involuntary sterilization." Proponents of the language contended that the addition of the word "directly" may make it more difficult for the President to certify that UNFPA supports coercive abortion programs in China. The language was ultimately defeated on September 6, 2007 through the adoption of an amendment introduced by Senator Sam Brownback during floor debate (S.Amdt 2707 to H.R. 2764). The amendment struck the committee language and inserted a previous version of the Kemp-Kasten amendment.

[28] Senate. H.R. 2764, Department of State, Foreign Operations and Related Programs Appropriations Act, 2008, 110th Congress, 1st session, Sec. 622, September 6, 2008.

[29] To read a transcript of the debate over Senator Boxer's amendment, see Congressional Record - Senate, 110th Congress, September 6, 2007, p. S11191.

[30] S.Amdt. 2719 to H.R. 2764, The Department of State, Foreign Operations, and Related Programs Appropriations Bill, FY2008, September 6, 2007.

[31] H.Amdt. 367 to H.R. 2764, June 21, 2007. The Mexico City policy denies U.S. funds to foreign NGOs that perform or promote abortion as a method of family planning, even if the activities are undertaken with non-U.S. funds.

[32] For more information on arguments made for and against the Lowey amendment by Members of Congress, see Congressional Record, U.S. House of Representatives, Vol. 153, No. 101, June 21, 2007, p. H6881-H6887, and Congressional Record, U.S. House of Representatives, Vol. 153, No. 101-Part II, June 21, 2007, pp. H6889-H6900.

[33] For the first four years of the Bush Administration, the budget request included a $25 million reserve for UNFPA funding in the International Organizations and Programs (IOP) account. However, the Administration's FY2006, FY2007, and FY2008 budget proposals did not set aside a reserve for UNFPA in the IOP account.

[34] is "White House: No U.N. Funding for China," *The Associated Press,* September 7, 2007.

In: Families: Rights, Laws and Stability
Editors: J. R. Redmund, K. B. Killigan, pp. 95-110 ISBN: 978-1-60456-203-3

Chapter 5

STATE FAMILY AND MEDICAL LEAVE LAWS*

Jon O. Shimabukuro, Cassandra LaNel Foley and Tara Alexandra Rainson

ABSTRACT

In 1993, Congress passed the Family and Medical Leave Act ("FMLA") to "balance the demands of the workplace with the needs of families." When the FMLA was enacted, it supplemented approximately 30 state statutes that provided some form of family and medical leave to employees who worked in those states. Although the FMLA and state family and medical leave laws are generally similar with regard to the availability of leave, they differ both in terms of coverage and scope. This article includes summaries of the family and medical leave laws of forty-five states and the District of Columbia. Laws pertaining to family and medical leave and maternity leave were not found in the codes of all 50 states. Summaries of the relevant leave statutes and regulations are organized in alphabetical order.

In 1993, Congress passed the Family and Medical Leave Act ("FMLA") to "balance the demands of the workplace with the needs of families."[1] Recognizing that many employees had to choose between parenting or caregiving and job security, Congress sought to enable employees to take "reasonable leave" for medical reasons, for the birth or adoption of a child, and for the care of a child, spouse, or parent with a serious health condition.[2]

When the FMLA was enacted, it supplemented approximately 30 state statutes that provided some form of family and medical leave to employees who worked in those states. Congress did not intend to preempt these laws.[3] Rather, Congress wanted to establish minimum standards for the availability of family and medical leave, particularly in states that did not have statutes extending such leave to their employees. Congress understood that more favorable leave benefits could be available under some state laws. Thus, section 401(b) of the FMLA indicates that nothing in the federal law "shall be construed to supersede any provision

* Excerpted from CRS Report RL33710, dated October 26, 2006.

of any State or local law that provides greater family or medical leave rights than the rights established under [the FMLA]."[4]

Although the FMLA and state family and medical leave laws are generally similar with regard to the availability of leave, they differ both in terms of coverage and scope. For example, under the FMLA and many of the state family and medical leave statutes and regulations, only certain employers are required to provide leave to their employees. The FMLA applies only to employers engaged in commerce or in an industry affecting commerce that have at least 50 employees who are employed for each working day during each of 20 or more calendar workweeks in the current or preceding calendar year.[5] In contrast, the state family and medical leave laws vary with regard to the number of employees who must be employed by an employer before it becomes subject to a law.[6]

The FMLA and state family and medical leave laws also differ with regard to scope. Section 102(a)(1) of the FMLA provides for a total of 12 workweeks of leave during any 12-month period for one or more of the following reasons:

> (1) Because of the birth of a son or daughter of the employee and in order to care for such son or daughter; (2) Because of the placement of a son or daughter with the employee for adoption or foster care; (3) In order to care for the spouse, or a son, daughter, or parent, of the employee, if such spouse, son, daughter, or parent has a serious health condition; (4) Because of a serious health condition that makes the employee unable to perform the functions of the position of such employee.[7]

In contrast, some state laws permit leave for reasons other than pregnancy, adoption, or a serious health condition.[8]

Forty-five states and the District of Columbia now appear to have family and medical leave laws. The following section provides citations and brief descriptions of the relevant laws. Many of the laws identified in this section govern state government employers. Title II of the FMLA amended the U. S. Code to add family and medical leave provisions to title 5 of the Code, the title that governs employees in the federal government. Under the Federal Employees Family Friendly Leave Act, federal employees are also entitled to use sick leave to care for a family member with an illness or injury, to make funeral arrangements for a family member, and to attend the funeral of a family member.[9]

State Family and Medical Leave Laws

Alabama

Ala. Code § 36-27-58 (2005): An Employees' Retirement System member may purchase up to one year's service credit in the system for any period of time while he or she was on maternity leave without pay.

Ala. Code § 16-1-18.1 (2005) and *Ala. Admin. Code r. 670-X-14-.01 (2006)*: State employees may take sick leave for personal illness, to care for a sick family member, for incapacitating personal injury, for the death of a family member, or for the death or serious illness of a non-family member with strong personal ties to the employee. Employees may accumulate an unlimited amount of sick leave at the rate of one day of leave per month of employment, and sick leave days may be transferred between employees. In case of serious illness, a permanent employee may be advanced an additional 24 days of sick leave.

Alaska

Alaska Stat. § 39.20.305 (2006): An officer or employee of the state who is otherwise qualified to take leave of absence may take family leave because of a serious health condition for a total of 18 workweeks during any 24-month period. An otherwise qualified officer or employee may take family leave because of pregnancy and childbirth or adoption for a total of 18 workweeks within a 12-month period. An eligible employee may take family leave for the birth or adoption of a child, to care for a child, spouse or parent with a serious health condition, or because of the employee's own health condition.

Arizona

Ariz. Rev. Stat. § 41-783 (2006): Personnel rules shall provide for the transfer of accumulated annual leave (1) between state employees in the same agency, or (2) between state employees in different agencies if the employees are members of the same family. Such transfers may occur if the employee to whom the leave is transferred has a seriously incapacitating and extended illness or injury or a member of the employee's immediate family has a seriously incapacitating and extended illness or injury and the employee has exhausted all available leave balances.

Ariz. Admin. Code § 2-5-404 (2005): A state employee may take sick leave for personal illness or for the illness of the employee's spouse, child, or parent. Sick leave may also be taken for a disability caused by pregnancy, childbirth, miscarriage, or abortion.

Ariz. Admin. Code § 2-5-411 (2005): With regard to state employees, "parental leave" means any combination of annual leave, sick leave, compensatory leave, or leave without pay taken by an employee due to pregnancy, childbirth, miscarriage, abortion, or adoption of children. Parental leave shall not exceed 12 weeks. An agency shall not require an employee to exhaust all annual leave, sick leave, or compensatory leave before taking leave without pay.

Arkansas

Ark. Code Ann. § 21-4-209 (2006): For public employees, maternity leave shall be treated as any other leave for sickness or disability. Accumulated sick leave and annual leave, if requested by the employee, shall be granted for maternity use, after which leave without pay may be used.

Ark. Code Ann. § 21-4-210 (2006): Public employees may be granted up to six months leave without pay for maternity and sick leave.

Ark. Code Ann. § 21-4-215 (2006): Public employees are entitled to up to seven days leave to serve as a bone marrow donor and up to 30 days leave to serve as an organ donor.

California

Cal. Gov't Code § 12945 (2006): Public employers and private employers with five or more employees must provide reasonable accommodations for conditions related to pregnancy and must allow an employee disabled by pregnancy, childbirth or related medical conditions to take up to four months of leave and return to work.

Cal. Gov't Code § 12945.2 (2006): Public employees and private employees in organizations with five or more workers who have more than 12 months of service and with at least 1,250 hours of service during the previous 12-month period must be allowed up to a total of 12 workweeks in any 12-month period for family care and medical leave. "Family care and medical leave" means any of the following: (1) leave for the birth of a child, the placement of a child with an employee for adoption or foster care, or the serious health condition of a child of the employee; (2) leave to care for a parent or a spouse who has a serious health condition; or (3) leave because of an employee's own serious health condition that makes the employee unable to perform the functions of the position of that employee, except for leave taken for disability on account of pregnancy, childbirth, or related medical conditions.

Cal. Gov't Code §§ 19991.6 and 19991.11 (2006): State employees are entitled to a year of leave without pay for pregnancy, 30 days leave with pay to be an organ donor, and five days leave without pay to be a bone marrow donor.

Cal. Lab. Code §§ 230.7 and 230.8 (2006): No employee may be discriminated against or discharged for visiting a child's school or day care facility.

Cal. Lab. Code § 233 (2006): Any employer who provides sick leave must allow sick leave to be used to attend to the illness of a child, spouse, parent, or domestic partner of the employee.

Colorado

Colo. Rev. Stat. § 19-5-211 (2005): An employer who permits paternity or maternity time off for the birth of a child must allow equal time off for the adoption of a child. If the employer has established a policy providing time off for biological parents, that period of time shall be the minimum period of leave available for adoptive parents. Any other benefits provided by the employer, such as job guarantee or pay or time off to care for a sick child, shall be available to both adoptive and biological parents on an equal basis.

Connecticut

Conn. Gen. Stat. §§ 5-248a and 5-248b (2006): Each permanent state employee shall be entitled to the following: (1) a maximum of 24 weeks of family leave of absence within any two-year period upon the birth or adoption of a child of such employee, or upon the serious illness of a child, spouse or parent of such employee; and (2) a maximum of twenty-four weeks of medical leave of absence within any two-year period upon the serious illness of such employee or in order for such employee to serve as an organ or bone marrow donor. Any such leave of absence shall be without pay.

Conn. Gen. Stat. § 31-51ll (2006): An employer of 75 or more employees must grant a total of 16 workweeks of leave during any 24-month period. Leave may be taken for the birth or adoption of a child; to care for a spouse, child or parent with a serious health condition; to serve as an organ or bone marrow donor; because of a serious health condition of the employee; or upon the placement of a child with the employee for foster care.

Conn. Gen. Stat. § 46a-60 (2006): Any state employer and any employer of three or more employees must allow a pregnant employee who takes leave because of her pregnancy to be reinstated to her original job or to an equivalent position.

Delaware

Del. Code Ann. tit. 29, § 5120 (2006): For child care purposes, a full-time or part-time employee of the state shall be allowed to use accumulated sick leave upon the birth of a child of the employee or the employee's spouse, or upon the adoption by the employee of a pre-kindergarten age child.

Del. Code. Ann. tit. 29, § 5116 (2006): An employee of the state is entitled to six weeks leave upon the adoption of a minor child.

District of Columbia

D.C. Code § 1-612.32 (2006): A voluntary transfer of leave is authorized when a potential recipient state employee will suffer a prolonged absence due to the employee's serious health condition or the employee's responsibility to provide personal care to an immediate relative.

D.C. Code §§ 32-501 and 32-502 (2006): A public or private employee is allowed 16 workweeks of family leave during any 24-month period for: (1) the birth of a child; (2) the placement of a child with the employee for adoption or foster care; (3) the placement of a child with the employee for whom the employee permanently assumes and discharges parental responsibility; or (4) the care of a family member of the employee who has a serious health condition.

D.C. Code § 32-503 (2006): A public or private employee who becomes unable to perform the functions of the employee's position because of a serious health condition shall be entitled to medical leave for as long as the employee is unable to perform the functions, except that the medical leave shall not exceed 16 workweeks during any 24-month period. The medical leave may be taken intermittently when medically necessary.

D.C. Code § 32-1202 (2006): Any public or private employee who is a parent shall be entitled to a total of 24 hours leave during any 12 month period to attend or participate in a school-related event for his or her child. Each agency or independent agency shall establish a voluntary leave transfer program under which accumulated leave may be transferred on an hour-for-hour basis within the agency to the leave account of any other eligible agency employee.

Florida

Fla. Stat. § 110.221 (2006): The state shall not: (1) terminate the employment of any employee in the career service because of pregnancy or the adoption of a child; (2) refuse to grant to a career service employee parental or family medical leave without pay for a period not to exceed six months; (3) deny a career service employee the use of and payment for annual leave credits for parental or family medical leave; (4) deny a career service employee the use of and payment for accrued sick leave or family sick leave for any reason deemed necessary by a physician or as established by policy. The statute also provides that upon returning at the end of parental or family medical leave of absence, the employee shall be reinstated to the same job or to an equivalent position with equivalent pay and with seniority, retirement, fringe benefits, and other service credits accumulated prior to the leave period.

Hawaii

Haw. Rev. Stat. § 398-3 (2006): Any public or private employee shall be entitled to a total of four weeks of family leave during any calendar year upon the birth or adoption of a child, or to care for the employee's child, spouse or reciprocal beneficiary, or parent with a serious health condition.

Idaho

Idaho Admin. Code § 15.04.01.242 (2005): The provisions of the federal Family and Medical Leave Act (FMLA) shall apply without regard to the exclusion for worksites employing less than fifty (50) employees in a seventy-five (75) mile area, and without the limitation on reinstatement of the highest-paid employees.

Idaho Admin. Code § 15.04.01.243 (2005): Pregnancy, childbirth, and related medical conditions are considered disabilities for sick leave purposes. Maternity and paternity leave for reasons other than disability shall be leave without pay unless the employee elects to use vacation time.

Illinois

5 Ill. Comp. Stat. Ann. 400/10 (2006): Public employees may participate in a sick leave bank to be used by any participating employee who has exhausted his or her accrued vacation time, personal days, sick leave and compensatory time. An employee may only use leave from the sick leave bank for the employee's personal catastrophic illness or injury.

5 Ill. Comp. Stat. Ann. 327/20 (2006): Public employees are entitled to up to 30 days per year to serve as organ or bone marrow donors. Leave is also available to donate blood or blood platelets.

820 Ill. Comp. Stat. Ann. 147/10, 147/15, and 147/40 (2006): Public employers and private employers of 50 or more people must grant eight hours per year per employee of school conference and activity leave related to the employee's child.

Indiana

Ind. Admin. Code tit. 31, r. 2-11-4, 2-11-4.5, and 2-11-8 (2006): State employees accumulate paid sick and personal leave.

Iowa

Iowa Code § 216.6 (2006): Public employees may take sick leave for disabilities caused by pregnancy, childbirth, miscarriage, and legal abortion. Where sufficient sick leave is not available, the employee may take up to an eight week leave of absence.

Kansas

Kan. Stat. Ann. § 75-5549 (2006): State employees may donate annual and sick leave to other state employees who are suffering from, or who have a family member suffering from, an extraordinary or severe illness, injury, impairment or physical or mental condition which has caused, or is likely to cause, the employee to take leave without pay or terminate employment. "Extraordinary or severe" means serious, extreme or life threatening.

Kan. Admin. Regs. §§ 1-9-5 and 1-9-6 (2006): State employees may use sick leave with pay for illness or disability, including pregnancy, childbirth, miscarriage, and abortion; the illness or disability, including pregnancy, childbirth, miscarriage, and abortion, of a family member; or for the adoption of a child or placement of a foster child. Employees may also receive up to one year of leave without pay for the same purposes.

Kentucky

Ky. Rev. Stat. Ann. § 18A.197 (2006): State employees with more than 75 hours sick leave may donate sick leave to other state employees who are suffering from, or have an immediate family member suffering from, a medically certified illness, injury, impairment, or physical or mental condition which has caused, or is likely to cause, the employee to go on leave for at least 10 consecutive working days. To qualify for a donation, an employee must have exhausted his or her accumulated sick leave, annual leave, and compensatory leave balances.

Ky. Rev. Stat. Ann § 337.015 (2006): Public and private employees may take up to six weeks leave for the adoption of a child under age seven.

Louisiana

La. Rev. Stat. Ann. §§ 23:341 and 23:342 (2006): Employers of 25 or more people are required to treat problems arising from pregnancy childbirth like any other temporary disability and to provide up to six weeks disability leave. Total pregnancy leave, including accrued vacation time, can be up to four months.

La. Rev. Stat. Ann. § 40:1299.124 (2006): Employers of 20 or more people shall grant up to 40 hours leave for bone marrow donation.

Maine

Me. Rev. Stat. Ann. tit. 26, § 636 (2005): Public employees and private employees of organizations that employ 25 or more people are entitled to 40 hours of leave in a 12 month period to care for a sick child, spouse, or parent.

Me. Rev. Stat. Ann. tit. 26, § 843 (2005): Public employees and private employees of organizations that employ 15 or more people are entitled to 10 weeks "family medical leave" for a serious health condition of the employee, child, or spouse; the birth or adoption of a child; or organ donation.

Maryland

Md. Code Ann., State Pers. and Pens. §§ 9-501 — 9-508 (2006): A state employee may use sick leave for personal illness, for the death or illness of an immediate family member, or for the birth or adoption of a child.

Md. Code Ann., State Pers. and Pens. § 9-1001 (2006): A state employee may use other available accrued leave concurrently with family and medical leave.

Md. Code Ann., State Pers. and Pens. § 9-1106 (2006): State employees are entitled to 30 days of leave to serve as an organ donor and seven days of leave to serve as a bone marrow donor.

Md. Code Ann., Lab. and Empl. § 3-802 (2006): An employer who provides paid leave following the birth of a child must provide the same leave following the adoption of a child.

Massachusetts

Mass Ann. Laws ch. 149, § 52D (2006): Public employers and private employers of 50 or more people must offer 24 hours of leave during any 12-month period, in addition to leave available under the federal Family and Medical Leave Act, to participate in a child's school activities, or to accompany a child or elderly relative to routine medical or dental appointments.

Mass. Ann. Laws ch. 149, § 105D (2006): State employers and private employers of six or more employees must allow eight weeks maternity leave for the birth or adoption of a child. Leave applies to the adoption of a child under 18 or a mentally or physically disabled child under 23.

Michigan

Mich. Comp. Laws § 38.1375 (2006): Public school employee may purchase service credits for maternity or paternity leave.

Minnesota

Minn. Stat. § 181.941 (2005): An employer of 21 or more employees must provide up to six weeks maternity leave following the birth or adoption of a child.

Minn. Stat. § 181.9412 (2005): Any Minnesota employer must allow employees 16 hours during any 12-month period to attend school conferences or school-related activities provided the conferences or school-related activities cannot be scheduled during nonwork hours. This provision also applies to the school activities of foster children.

Minn. Stat. § 181.9413 (2005): An employer of 21 or more employees must allow the use of personal sick leave to care for a sick child.

Mississippi

Miss. Code Ann. § 25-3-95 (2006): Public employees may use major medical leave for the injury or illness of an immediate family member. Any employee may donate a portion of his or her earned personal leave or major medical leave to another employee who is suffering from a catastrophic injury or illness, or to another employee who has a member of his or her immediate family who is suffering from a catastrophic injury or illness.

Missouri

Mo. Rev. Stat. § 105.271 (2006): Public employees may use the same leave granted to biological parents upon the birth of a child to adopt a child and may use the same leave granted to biological parents to care for a sick child to care for a sick adopted child or stepchild.

Montana

Mont. Code Ann. § 2-18-606 (2005): State employees are entitled to up to 15 days of leave for the birth or adoption of a child.

Mont. Code Ann. § 49-2-101(11) (2005): "Employer" means an employer of one or more persons or an agent of the employer but does not include a fraternal, charitable, or religious association or corporation if the association or corporation is not organized either for private profit or to provide accommodations or services that are available on a nonmembership basis.

Mont. Code Ann. § 49-2-310 (2005): An employer must grant to the employee a reasonable leave of absence for pregnancy; and must allow an employee disabled as a result of pregnancy to use accrued disability or leave benefits.

Nebraska

Neb. Rev. Stat. § 48-234 (2006): An employee who offers maternity leave for the birth of a child must also provide leave for the adoption of a child.

Nevada

Nev. Rev. Stat. § 613.335 (2006): An employer who offers sick leave must offer leave for pregnancy, miscarriage and childbirth.

New Hampshire

N.H. Rev. Stat. Ann. § 100-A:9-a (2006): Any member of the New Hampshire retirement system who is on leave under the provisions of the federal Family and Medical Leave Act of 1993 shall be considered in service for purposes of eligibility for death or disability benefits.

New Jersey

N.J. Stat. Ann. § 34:11B-3 (2006): A private or public employer of 50 or more employees shall provide family leave to employees who been employed for 1,000 base hours during the immediately preceding 12-month period.

N.J. Stat. Ann. § 34:11B-4 (2006): An employee shall be entitled to 12 weeks of leave in any 24-month period. Leave may be paid, unpaid or a combination of paid and unpaid. If an employer provides paid family leave for fewer than 12-workweeks, the additional weeks of leave added to attain the 12-workweek total may be unpaid.

New York

N.Y. Lab. Law. § 201-c (2006): Whenever an employer or governmental agency permits leave for the birth of a child, an adoptive parent shall be entitled to the same leave.

N.Y. Lab. Law. § 202-a (2006): A public or private who employs 20 or more employees must grant leave for the donation of bone marrow to an employee who works for an average of 20 or more hours per week.

N.Y. Lab. Law. § 202-b (2006): Any state employee shall be allowed up to seven days paid leave to donate bone marrow and up to 30 days paid leave to serve as an organ donor. Such leave shall be in addition to any other sick or annual leave allowed.

N.Y. Workers' Comp. Law § 201(9) (2006): A private employers' disability benefits shall also include pregnancy.

North Carolina

N.C. Gen. Stat. § 95-28.3 (2006): An employer shall grant 4 hours of leave for the employee's involvement in his/her child's school. An employer is not required to pay for leave.

North Dakota

N.D. Cent. Code § 54-06-14.1 (2006): State employees who suffer from or has a relative or household member suffering from an extraordinary or severe illness may use shared leave, including both annual and sick leave, that shall not exceed four months in any 12-month period.

N.D. Cent. Code §54-06-14.2 (2006): State employees who suffer from an extraordinary or severe illness may use shared leave, including both annual and sick leave, that shall not exceed four months in any 12-month period.

N.D. Cent. Code § 54-06-14.4 (2006): The state may grant leave of absence, not to exceed 20 workdays for the donation of an organ or bone marrow. An employee may use donated annual leave or sick leave. The state may grant a paid leave for the up to 20-workdays.

N.D. Cent. Code § 54-52.4-01 (2006): A state employee shall be entitled to family leave if employed for at least 12-months, and has worked at least 1,250 hours over the previous 12-months.

N.D. Cent. Code § 54-52.4-02 (2006): A state employer shall grant family leave for the care of a child (includes adopted or foster) within 12-months of the child's birth or placement; the care of a child, spouse, or parent with a serious health condition; or because of the employee's serious health condition. An employee may take leave in any 12-month period for not more than 12-workweeks. Leave is not required to be granted with pay.

N.D. Cent. Code § 54-52.4-03 (2006): A state employer that provides leave for its employees for illnesses or other medical or health reasons shall grant an employee's request to use that leave to care for the employee's child, spouse, or parent with a serious health condition. An employee may take not more than 40 hours of leave in any 12 month period. The employer shall compensate the employee for leave.

Ohio

Ohio Rev. Code Ann. § 124.136 (2006): State permanent full-time and part-time employees who work 30 or more hours per week may be eligible for parental leave and benefits upon the birth or adoption of a child. Employees may elect to receive $2,000 for adoption expenses in lieu of receiving the paid leave benefit. Parental leave shall not exceed 6 continuous weeks. Use of parental leave does not prohibit taking leave under the "Family and Medical Leave Act of 1993."

Oklahoma

Okla. Stat. tit. 74, § 840-2.23 (2005): An eligible state employee who is suffering from an extraordinary illness or condition, has experienced the death of a relative or household member, or is affected by a presidentially declared national disaster may participate in the state leave sharing program. An employee may use up to 261 days of donated leave during total state employment. An employee suffering from a terminal illness may receive up to 365 days of donated leave during total state employment.

Oregon

Or. Rev. Stat. § 659A.153 (2006): A public or private employer of 25 or more persons during each of 20 or more calendar workweeks is required to grant family leave to eligible employees.

Or. Rev. Stat. § 659A.156 (2006): An employee shall have worked 180 days or 25 hours per week during the 180 days immediately before the date on which the family leave would commence.

Or. Rev. Stat. § 659A.159 (2006): Leave taken for the care of an infant/newly adopted child/newly placed foster child/adopted or foster child more than 18 years old must be completed within 12 months after birth or placement of child.

Or. Rev. Stat. § 659A.162 (2006): An eligible employee is entitled to up to 12 weeks of family leave within any one-year period. In addition, a female employee may take a total of 12 weeks within any one-year period for an illness, injury or condition related to pregnancy or childbirth. An employee may take an additional 12 weeks of leave within one year to care for a sick child.

Or. Rev. Stat. § 659A.312 (2006): An employer shall grant already accrued paid leave to an employee for the donation of bone marrow. The leave shall not exceed accrued paid leave or 40 work hours, whichever is less. An employee shall have worked an average of 20 or more hours per week.

Rhode Island

R.I. Gen. Laws § 28-48-1 (2006): A private employer of 50 or more employees and a public employer of 30 or more employees are required to grant parental and family leave.

R.I. Gen. Laws § 28-48-2 (2006): An employee who has been employed for 12 consecutive months shall be entitled to 13 weeks of parental or family leave in any 2 calendar years. Leave may consist of paid and unpaid leave.

R.I. Gen. Laws § 28-48-11 (2006): An employer who allows sick time or sick leave to be utilized after the birth of a child shall allow the same time for the adoption placement of a child 16 years of age or less.

R.I. Gen. Laws § 28-48-13 (2006): An employee shall be entitled to 10 hours during 12 months to attend school conferences or other school-related activities for a child. The employee is not entitled to paid leave; except accrued paid leave.

South Carolina

S.C. Code Ann. § 8-11-40 (2005): Eligible full-time state employees are entitled to 15 days' sick leave a year with pay. Eligible part-time state employees are entitled to sick leave prorated on the basis of 15 days a year. Employees may use no more than 10 days of sick leave annually to care for ill members of their immediate families.

S.C. Code Ann. § 8-11-65 (2005): A public employee who wishes to be an organ donor and who accrues annual or sick leave is entitled to leave of up to 30 days in a fiscal year.

S.C. Code Ann. § 8-11-155 (2005): A state adoptive parent may use up to six weeks of accrued sick leave to care for a child after placement.

S.C. Code Ann. §§ 8-11-700 and 8-11-710 (2005): State employees may request leave from the pool leave account for a personal emergency.

S.C. Code Ann. § 44-43-80 (2005): A private or public employer of 20 or more employees may grant paid leave for the donation of bone marrow. An employee who works an average of 20 or more hours a week may request paid leave not to exceed 40 work hours.

South Dakota

S.D. Codified Laws § 3-6-7 (2006): An eligible state employee may use up to five days for sick leave for personal emergency. Adoption of a child is treated as natural childbirth for leave purposes.

S.D. Codified Laws § 3-6-8 (2006): Sick leave, not exceeding 28 days, may be advanced to an employee who has used up all of his accumulated and earned leave.

S.D. Codified Laws § 3-6-10 (2006): Employees may take leave without pay.

Tennessee

Tenn. Code Ann. § 4-21-408 (2005): Full time employees of private and public employers with 100 full-time employees may be absent for up to four months for adoption, pregnancy, childbirth and nursing an infant. Leave may be with or without pay.

Tenn. Code Ann. § 8-50-802 (2005): Sick leave may be granted to a state officer or employee who is scheduled to work 1,600 hours or more in a fiscal year. Sick leave for maternity or paternity shall not exceed the accumulated sick leave balance or 30 working days, whichever is less.

Tenn. Code Ann. § 8-50-806 (2005): Adoptive parents are granted a special 30-day leave. An employee may use sick leave for all or a portion of that 30 days, not to exceed the employee's leave balance if the child is one year old or less.

Tenn. Code Ann. § 8-50-905 (2005): An eligible state employee may participate in the sick leave bank.

Tenn. Code Ann. § 8-50-907 (2005): Participants in the sick leave bank may be granted up to 90 days of leave.

Texas

Texas Gov't Code Ann. § 661.004 (2006): An eligible state employee may use time in the sick leave pool for a catastrophic illness/injury.

Texas Gov't Code Ann. § 661.006 (2006): An employee may also withdraw time in the case of catastrophic illness or injury of an immediate family member. Time withdrawn shall not exceed the lesser of 1/3 of the total time in the pool or 90 days.

Texas Gov't Code Ann. § 661.206 (2006): A state employee may use up to 8 hours of sick leave to attend parent-teacher conferences.

Texas Gov't Code Ann. § 661.902 (2006): A state employee is entitled to emergency leave without a deduction in salary because of death in the family.

Texas Gov't Code Ann. § 661.906 (2006): A state employee is entitled to leave without a deduction in salary for attending meetings regarding a foster child.

Texas Gov't Code Ann. § 661.909 (2006): A state employer may grant leave without pay. Leave may not exceed 12-months.

Texas Gov't Code Ann. § 661.910 (2006): A disabled state employee is entitled to leave without deduction in salary for attending a dog training program. The leave may not exceed 10 working days in a fiscal year.

Texas Gov't Code Ann. § 661.912 (2006): A state employee with 12 months of service and 1,250 work hours is entitled to leave under the Family and Medical Leave Act of 1993.

Texas Gov't Code Ann. § 661.913 (2006): A state employee who has been employed for fewer than 12 months or who worked fewer than 1,250 hours during the 12-month period preceding the beginning of leave is eligible to take parental leave of absence not to exceed 12 weeks for the birth of a natural child or adoption or foster care placement of a child younger than three years of age. The employee must first use all available and applicable vacation and sick leave while taking the leave, and the remainder of the leave is unpaid.

Vermont

Vt. Stat. Ann. tit. 21, § 471 (2006): Parental leave requirements apply to a private and public employer of 10 or more individuals who are employed for an average of 30 hours per week during a year. Family leave requirements apply to private and public employers of 15 or more individuals who are employed for an average of 30 hours per week during a year.

Vt. Stat. Ann. tit. 21, § 472 (2006): An employee, during any 12-month period, shall be entitled to take unpaid leave not to exceed 12 weeks for parental or family leave. The employee may use accrued sick, vacation, or other accrued paid leave, not to exceed six weeks.

Vt. Stat. Ann. tit. 21, § 472a (2006): In addition, an employee shall be entitled to take unpaid leave not to exceed 4 hours in any 30-day period and not to exceed 24 hours in any 12-month period to attend a child's school activities; family member's medical/dental or professional services appointments; and to respond to a child's medical emergency.

Virginia

Va. Code Ann. § 51.1-1107 (2006): Eligible state employees shall receive a calculated amount of family and personal leave based on the number of months of state service.

Va. Code Ann. § 51.1-1108 (2006): Eligible state employees can take family and personal leave for short-term incident, illness or death of a family member, or other personal need. Employers shall compensate employees 100% for each hour taken, not to exceed the employee's family and personal leave balance.

Va. Code Ann. § 51.1-1110 (2006): Short-term disability benefits shall be payable only during periods of total disability, partial disability, maternity leave, or periodic absences due to a major chronic condition.

Washington

Wash. Rev. Code § 41.04.665 (2006): A state employee shall not receive more than 260 days leave from the leave sharing program.

Wash. Rev. Code § 49.78 (2006): An employee is entitled to 12 workweeks of leave during any 12-month period. Leave granted may consist of unpaid leave. Leave may consist of paid and unpaid leave. In addition the employee is entitled to leave for sickness or temporary disability because of pregnancy or childbirth.

Wash. Rev. Code § 49.78.020 (2006): A private or public employer of 50 or more employees is required to provide medical and family leave.

West Virginia

W. Va. Code § 21-5D-3 (2006): A state employer is not prohibited from providing employees with rights to family leave which are more generous.

W. Va. Code § 21-5D-4 (2006): An employee shall be entitled to 12 weeks of unpaid family leave, following the exhaustion of all annual and personal leave, during any 12-month period.

W. Va. Code § 29-6-28 (2006): A full-time state employee shall receive up to 120 hours of paid leave for donation of a liver or kidney. A full-time state employee shall receive up to 56 hours of paid leave for the donation of bone marrow.

Wisconsin

Wis. Stat. § 103.10 (2006): Family leave applies to private employers of 50 or more individuals on a permanent basis and to a state employer. The employee shall have been employed for at least 1,000 hours during the preceding 52-week period. In a 12-month period, an employee may take six weeks for the birth or adoption placement of a child; two weeks to care for a family member; or eight weeks for any combination of reasons. No employee may take more than two weeks of medical leave during a 12-month period. An employee may use paid or unpaid leave.

Wis. Stat. § 230.35 (2006): A state employer shall grant 5 workdays of leave to a bone marrow donor. A state employer shall grant 30 workdays of leave to a human organ donor. An employee shall receive his or her base state pay without interruption during the leave of absence.

REFERENCES

[1] 29 U.S.C. § 2601 *et seq.*
[2] *See* 29 U.S.C. § 2601(b)(2).
[3] *See* S.Rept. 103-3, at 38 (1993).
[4] 29 U.S.C. § 2651(b).
[5] 29 U.S.C. § 2611(4)(I). *See also* 29 U.S.C. § 2611(2)(B)(ii) (Employers who employ 50 or more employees within a 75-mile radius of an employee's worksite are subject to the FMLA even if they may have fewer than 50 employees at a single worksite.).
[6] For example, in Montana, an employer of just one individual is subject to the relevant state law. Alternately, the Oregon family and medical leave statute applies to an employer of 25 or more employees during each of 20 or more calendar workweeks.
[7] 29 U.S.C. § 2612(a)(1).
[8] For example, under Rhode Island law, an employee is entitled to 10 hours of unpaid leave during a 12-month period to attend a child's school conferences or other school-related activities. Similarly, under Louisiana law, employers of 20 or more individuals shall grant up to 40 hours of leave for bone marrow donation.
[9] *See* 5 U.S.C. § 6307.

In: Families: Rights, Laws and Stability ISBN: 978-1-60456-203-3
Editors: J. R. Redmund, K. B. Killigan, pp. 111-118

Chapter 6

EVEN START FAMILY LITERACY PROGRAMS: AN OVERVIEW*

Gail McCallion

ABSTRACT

The Even Start program provides education and related services jointly to parents lacking a high school diploma (or equivalent) and their young children. Even Start services include basic academic instruction and parenting skills training for the adults, and early childhood education for their children, along with necessary supplementary services such as child care or transportation. Generally, Even Start programs do not directly provide all of these services; rather, they establish networks of service providers, including Head Start programs and grantees under the Adult Education Act (AEA). Even Start is the only federal program specifically dedicated to providing services to both disadvantaged young children and their parents.

The families served by Even Start programs are highly disadvantaged, with very low levels of education and income, and increasing proportions of them have limited English language skills.

The Even Start program was reauthorized in the 106th Congress, in P.L. 106-554, the Departments of Labor, Health and Human Services, Education, and Related Agencies Appropriations Act for FY2001. ESEA Title I, Part B was renamed the William F. Goodling Even Start Family Literacy Programs and was reauthorized for five years beginning with an authorization of $250 million for FY2001. The reauthorizing language is largely the same as language contained in the Literacy Involves Families Together Act, H.R. 3222 (Goodling), which was passed by the full House on September 12, 2000. However, language in H.R. 3222 specifying that religious organizations should be treated the same as other nongovernmental organizations in the awarding of subgrants *was not* included in the final reauthorization language.

P.L. 107-110 (the No Child Left Behind Act of 2001), the Elementary and Secondary Education Act reauthorization legislation, which was signed into law on January 8, 2002, moved the William F. Goodling Even Start Family Literacy Programs from Title I Part B of the ESEA to Subpart 3 of Title I Part B of the No Child Left Behind Act and extended the authorization period through FY2007. The only change to the program was an

* Excerpted from CRS Report RL30448, dated September 25, 2006.

amendment allowing states to use funds for state-level activities to improve the quality of family literacy services provided (in addition to other previously authorized uses).

The Even Start program's funding was reduced to $99 million for FY2006 (including the FY2006 across-the-board reduction). For FY2007, the Administration has requested no funding for the program, the House Committee on Appropriations has recommended $70 million in funding for the program, and the Senate Committee on Appropriations has recommended no funding for the program.

MAJOR PROVISIONS OF EVEN START

The Even Start Family Literacy program, authorized by ESEA Title I, Part B, provides education and related services jointly to disadvantaged parents and their young children. The purpose of the program is to integrate early childhood education, adult basic education, and parenting skills education into a "unified family literacy program" (ESEA Section 1201). An assumption underlying Even Start is that children whose parents have low literacy or basic education levels are more likely to be educationally successful if, in addition to receiving early childhood instruction themselves, their parents receive educational services plus instruction in how to help their children learn. Further, parents may be more motivated to participate in adult basic education programs if one of the purposes of such education is to support their children's educational development. While some other federal education programs — such as ESEA Title I, Part A programs — also provide services to both disadvantaged young children and their parents, Even Start is the only federal program specifically dedicated to this purpose.

Under the Even Start legislation, the U.S. Department of Education (ED) is authorized to make grants to states for assistance to eligible entities — consisting of a local educational agency (LEA) in collaboration with a community based organization, institution of higher education, or other agency or nonprofit organization — for joint programs of education for children aged 0-7 years[1] and their parents. In each participating family, at least one parent must be eligible to be served under the Adult Education Act (AEA) — i.e., not enrolled in school and not a high school graduate (or equivalent) — or, if a LEA provides the basic education component of the program, services may be provided to parents who are within the compulsory school age range for their state.

Even Start program services *must* include adult literacy instruction, early childhood education, instruction to help parents support their child's education, recruitment, screening of parents, staff training, and home-based instruction. In addition, child care and transportation services *may* be provided, *if* these services are necessary and other funding sources are not available. Typically, Even Start programs do not directly provide all of these services, rather they establish networks of service providers, including Head Start programs and grantees under the AEA.

Even Start programs must be coordinated with other programs with similar purposes, operate year-round, and be independently evaluated.

Five percent of Even Start funds is reserved for programs serving migrant children plus the outlying areas and Indian tribes;[2] and up to 3% is reserved for a national evaluation, technical assistance, and program improvement. Remaining appropriations provide Even Start grants to the states in proportion to ESEA Title I, Part A grants,[3] with a state minimum of the greater of 0.5% of all grants, or $250,000.

Up to 6% of state grants may be used for state administration and technical assistance.[4] Local grants are made by state educational agencies (SEAs) based on recommendations by a review panel, consisting of an early childhood education specialist, an adult education specialist, and at least one additional member. Programs are to be in areas with high rates of poverty, illiteracy, unemployment, limited English proficiency, or disadvantaged children. Even Start grants are to be made for a period of up to four years, and may be renewed for up to four additional years. States receiving Even Start grants are required to develop "indicators of program quality," to be used to monitor and improve Even Start programs in the state, and to determine whether to continue funding local programs. P.L. 106-554, Title XVI, requires states to submit to ED their quality indicators for Even Start programs to be eligible for continued funding under the program. The federal share is generally limited to 90% for the first year, declining to 50% for the fifth, sixth and seventh years, and 35% for subsequent years.[5] The federal share limitation may be waived if an entity would not otherwise be able to participate.

Funding for the Even Start program grew from $14,820,000 in FY1989, the program's initial year, to $225,094,720 for FY2005 (including the FY2005 across-the-board reduction). The program's funding was significantly reduced to $99,000,000 in FY2006.[6] See table 1. for the program's complete funding history. This decrease in funding is likely to continue in FY2007. For FY2007, the Administration has requested no funding, the House Committee on Appropriations has recommended $70 million in funding, and the Senate Committee on Appropriations has recommended no funding.

Table 1. Even Start Funding: 1989-2006

1989	$14,820,000
1990	$24,201,000
1991	$49,770,000
1992	$70,000,000
1993	$89,123,000
1994	$91,373,000
1995	$102,024,000
1996	$101,997,000
1997	$101,992,000
1998	$124,000,000
1999	$135,000,000
2000	$150,000,000
2001	$250,000,000
2002	$250,000,000
2003	$248,375,000
2004	$246,910,000
2005	$225,095,000
2006	$99,000,000

Source: U.S. Department of Education Justifications of Appropriations Estimates to the Congress.
Note: These amounts are not adjusted for price level changes.

PROGRAM PARTICIPANTS, SERVICES, AND OUTCOMES

Participants

Even Start has grown from 76 local programs serving approximately 2,500 families in 1989-1990 to 855 programs serving approximately 32,000 families in 2000-2001.[7] The most recent available data (2000-2001) are based on program data for a period prior to changes required in the 2000 reauthorization of Even Start. These data indicate that Even Start programs tend to target families with children under age 5; 40% of participating children were 0-2 years old and 28% were 3-4 years old. The parents in the families served generally have low levels of education; for example in 2000-2001, 44% of parents had a 9th grade or less level of education upon entering the program. Further, the income of participating families is typically quite low — 84% of families had income below the federal poverty level. Only 23% of participating parents in 2000-2001 were employed.[8] The share of participants who are Hispanic was 46% in 2000-2001, while 30% were white, 19% were African American, and the remaining 7% were Asian, Native American, Hawaiian, or Multi-Racial. The percentage of participants from non-English-language backgrounds is high — 45% of new Even Start enrollees speak English as a second language. The top four reasons given by parents for enrolling in Even Start were a desire to improve their educational status (get a GED), their parenting skills, their ability to be a better teacher of their child, and their children's chance of future school success.

Services Provided

In most cases, Even Start programs do not directly provide all of the required services; rather they coordinate and integrate services provided by other agencies, especially early childhood education provided by Head Start or state preschool programs, or adult basic education provided by AEA grantees. The services most often provided directly by Even Start programs are early childhood education and parenting skills education. In addition to the core services that all Even Start programs must provide, the support services most often provided are child care, meals, transportation, and social services.

The average federal budget for Even Start programs surveyed in 2000-2001 was $175,439. The average federal Even Start program expenditures per participating family was $4,708 in 2000-2001. The rates of actual participation in various Even Start activities by the families being served in 2000-2001 were 84% for adult education, 89% for parenting education and parent-child joint activities, and 95% for early childhood education; with 82% of families participating in all core services. Maintaining the intensity of services and rates of participation continue to be an issue — about half of the Even Start families who joined Even Start between 1997-1998 and 2000-2001 left the program within 10 months. In 2000-2001, 17% of families who left Even Start did so because they had completed their education goals under the program. The majority of participants who left did so because of job conflicts, relocation, motivational issues, and other concerns (such as poor health, homelessness, etc.).

Evidence from the research literature has indicated that children who participate in intensive high-quality services score higher on literacy measures.[9] And, evidence from national Even Start evaluations has indicated that families participate more when more intensive services are offered. As a consequence Even Start projects have increased the amount of early childhood education and adult education services offered. However, most Even Start parents do not use all the hours of services available for themselves and their children. For example, in 2000-2001, on average, children birth to two received 30% of the service hours made available. For children aged 3 and 4, 5, and school-aged, the averages were 37%, 44%, and 62%, respectively.

Outcomes

The most recent national Even Start evaluation, for 2000-2001, was based on two data sources — an experimental design study (EDS) that tracked 18 projects that agreed to randomly assign new families to Even start or a control group; and, the Even Start Performance Information Reporting System (ESPIRS) which tracks annual data from the universe of Even Start projects. Although families participating in the EDS were randomly assigned to control and Even Start groups, the 18 projects participating were not randomly selected. The EDS families were more likely than Even Start families as a whole to be Hispanic (75% versus 46%), and to be participating in Even Start projects in urban areas (83% versus 55%).

The national evaluation collected data on 41 different outcome measures for the families participating in the EDS. The results indicated that the Even Start children and their parents did not perform better than the control group children and their parents. Even Start children and their parents made gains in literacy and other measures, but so did control group parents and children:

> The data show that children and parents in the control group made the same kinds of gains on literacy assessments, on parent reports of child literacy, on parent-child reading, on literacy resources at home, on family economic self-sufficiency, and so on, that were seen for Even Start families.[10]

The only area in which Even Start children did significantly better than control group children was in teacher reports of behavior problems for elementary school aged children.

LEGISLATION

P.L. 107-110 (the No Child Left Behind Act of 2001), the Elementary and Secondary Education Act reauthorization legislation, which was signed into law on January 8, 2002, moved the William F. Goodling Even Start Family Literacy Programs from Title I Part B of the ESEA, to Subpart 3 of Title I Part B of the No Child Left Behind Act of 2001. The only change to the program was an amendment allowing states to use funds for state-level activities to improve the quality of family literacy services provided (in addition to other previously authorized uses).

The Even Start program was reauthorized in the 106th Congress in H.R. 4577, the Departments of Labor, Health and Human Services, Education, and Related Agencies

Appropriations Act for FY2001, signed into law as P.L. 106-554. ESEA Title I, Part B was renamed the William F. Goodling Even Start Family Literacy Programs, and was reauthorized for five years beginning with an authorization of $250 million for FY2001. The reauthorizing language is largely the same as language contained in the Literacy Involves Families Together Act, H.R. 3222 (Goodling), which was passed by the full House on September 12, 2000. However, language in H.R. 3222 specifying that religious organizations should be treated the same as other nongovernmental organizations in the awarding of subgrants *was not* included in the final reauthorization language. In addition, the Inexpensive Book Distribution Program was not moved to the Even Start program in H.R. 4577; state grants for state administration and technical assistance were increased from 5% to 6% (grants for administration may not exceed half of the total); and states are required to submit to ED their quality indicators for Even Start programs to be eligible for continued funding under the program.

The Literacy Involves Families Together Act, H.R. 3222 (Goodling), was introduced in the House on November 4, 1999 and referred to the House Committee on Education and the Workforce. H.R. 3222 was reported by the full Committee on February 29, 2000; it was passed by the full House on September 12, 2000. H.R. 3222 proposed authorizing $250 million in funding for Even Start for FY2001, and proposed to:

- Rename Section 1202, Part B: "The William F. Goodling Even Start Family Literacy Programs";
- Require more stringent qualifications and standards for staff paid out of Even Start funds;
- Permit Even Start programs to serve children aged 8 or older if services are provided in collaboration with ESEA Title I, Part A programs;
- Authorize states to use a share of their grants to improve the quality of services provided by local grantees whose services have been of low quality, and to permit states to provide technical assistance to help local programs of demonstrated effectiveness to "access and leverage additional funds";
- Require grantees to use instructional programs "based on scientifically based reading research" for children (including reading readiness activities for preschool children), and if possible, for adults;
- Would have added to the list of indicators of an area's need for a program: whether an area has a high percentage of parents who have been victims of domestic violence, or who are receiving assistance under a state program funded under Part A of Title IV of the Social Security Act; ! reserve not more than 3% of funds appropriated for Even Start to provide technical assistance to, and to carry out an independent evaluation of, programs receiving Even Start assistance;
- Increase the amount of funds reserved for migrant programs, outlying areas and Indian tribes from 5% to 6%, if the amount appropriated for the program exceeds $200 million;
- Specify that no state shall award a subgrant for less than $52,500 in the ninth and subsequent years;
- Provide for a one-time coordination grant for each eligible state in the amount of: the lesser of $1 million or the amount the appropriation for Even Start exceeds the previous year's appropriation;

- Require Even Start programs to employ "continuing use of evaluation data for program improvement," and to provide information on how their plan "provides for rigorous and objective evaluation of progress toward" meeting the program's stated objectives;
- Reserve, in years in which the current year's appropriation for Even Start exceeds that of the previous year: "the lesser of $2 million or 50% of the increase in total Even Start appropriations each year" to be used by the National Institute for Literacy to conduct, through "an entity ... that has expertise in carrying out longitudinal studies of the development of literacy skills in children": scientifically based reading research on adult literacy and helping parents support the literacy development of their children;
- Move the Inexpensive Book Distribution Program from ESEA Title X, Part E, and add it as Title II under this act; with an authorization of $20 million;
- Amend the definition of an eligible entity to include "a religious organization." Specify that religious organizations shall be treated the same as other nongovernmental organizations in the awarding of subgrants, but an Even Start program may not subject a participant to "sectarian worship or instruction or proselytization."
- Provide that no services may be "provided by voucher or certificate" and, that "for purposes of any Federal, State or local law, receipt of financial assistance under this part of Section [1029(b)] shall constitute receipt of Federal financial assistance or aid."

On January 19, 1999, the Educational Opportunities Act, S. 2 (Jeffords), was introduced in the Senate and referred to the Committee on Health, Education, Labor and Pensions. S. 2 was reported by the full Committee on April 12, 2000. This bill would have, among other things, authorized $500 million for Even Start for FY2001 and would have amended Even Start to:

- Permit Even Start programs to serve children aged 8 or older in collaboration with ESEA Title I, Part A programs;
- Authorize states to use a share of their grants to improve the quality of services provided by local grantees;
- Require the use of instructional methods "based on scientifically based reading research" for children and, if possible, for adults;
- Reserve up to 3% of funds for technical assistance and an independent evaluation;
- Increase the funds reserved for migrants outlying areas and Indians from 5% to 6%, if appropriations exceed $250 million; and
- Require Even Start programs to "use methods to ensure that participating families successfully complete the program"; and
- Require each state that wishes to receive an Even Start grant to submit a plan specifying indicators of program quality and the state's plan for ensuring each funded program fully implements Even Start requirements, describe how the state will conduct subgrant competitions, and describe how it will coordinate resources to improve statewide family literacy services.

REFERENCES

[1] Title XVI of P.L. 106-554 (the Departments of Labor, Health and Human Services, Education, and Related Agencies Appropriations Act for FY2001) permits the program to serve children 8 or older if services are provided in collaboration with ESEA Title I, Part A program.

[2] The reservation is *six percent* if appropriations are more than $200 million.

[3] ESEA Title I, Part A grants are made primarily in proportion to school age (5-17 years) children in poor families multiplied by a state expenditure factor. For more information on the Title I, Part A allocation formulas, see CRS Report RL31487, *Education for the Disadvantaged: Overview of Title I-A Amendments Under the No Child Left Behind Act*, by Wayne Riddle.

[4] Increased from 5% to 6% by P.L. 106-554, Title XVI (Grants for administration may not exceed half of the total).

[5] Even Start Amendments contained in the Omnibus Appropriations Act for FY2000 (P.L. 106-113), removed the eight-year limitation on the duration of awards, and reduced the federal share of Even Start grants to 35% for the ninth and subsequent years. P.L. 106-113 also amended Even Start to require SEAs to start progress reviews after the *first* year of receipt of subgrant funds.

[6] CRS Report RL33071, *Even Start: Funding Controversy*, by Gail McCallion.

[7] Data included here are from the *Third National Even Start Evaluation*, 2003, prepared for the U.S. Department of Education, Planning and Evaluation Service.

[8] Nevertheless most of their income comes from wages, although not from the non wage-earning parent participating in Even Start.

[9] W. Steven Barnett, "Long-term Effects of Early Childhood Programs on Cognitive and School Outcomes," *Long-term Outcomes of Early Childhood Programs* [The Future of Children], vol. 5, no. 3, pp. 25-50.

[10] Third National Even Start Evaluation, p. 165.

In: Families: Rights, Laws and Stability ISBN: 978-1-60456-203-3
Editors: J. R. Redmund, K. B. Killigan, pp. 119-127

Chapter 7

POTENTIAL EFFECT OF MARRIAGE ON SUPPLEMENTAL SECURITY INCOME (SSI) ELIGIBILITY AND BENEFITS*

Scott Szymendera

ABSTRACT

Supplemental Security Income (SSI) is a major benefit program for low-income persons with disabilities and senior citizens. As a means tested program, SSI places income and resource limits on individuals and married couples for the purposes of determining their eligibility and level of benefits. To become and remain eligible to receive SSI benefits, single individuals may not have countable resources valued at more than $2,000 and married couples may not have countable resources valued at more than $3,000. Although a person's home and car are excluded from these calculations, most other assets owned by a person or married couple are counted and in most cases, the assets of both partners in a marriage are considered shared and equally available to both the husband and the wife.

A person's countable income must be below SSI program guidelines to qualify for benefits and a person's monthly benefit level is reduced by a portion of his or her earned and unearned income. The income of a person ineligible for SSI can be considered when calculating the benefit amount of that person's spouse. A complicated process of deeming is used to determine how much of the ineligible person's income is to be considered when calculating his or her spouse's monthly SSI benefits.

In some cases marriage may result in a person being denied SSI benefits or seeing his or her SSI benefit level reduced because of the increase in family income or assets that results from the marriage. This can occur if an SSI beneficiary marries another SSI beneficiary or a person not in the SSI program. This potential effect of marriage on the SSI eligibility and benefits of SSI beneficiaries has been called a "marriage penalty" by the National Council on Disability.

This article provides an overview of the potential effect of a marriage to another SSI recipient or an ineligible person on an individual's eligibility for and level of SSI

* Excerpted from CRS Report RL33675, dated May 2, 2007.

benefits. Examples of cases in which a marriage can reduce a person's SSI benefits are provided. To date, no legislation has been introduced in the 110th Congress that would change the way marriage can affect SSI eligibility and benefits. This article will be updated to reflect any legislative changes.

This article provides an overview of the potential effects of marriage on Supplemental Security Income (SSI) eligibility and benefits. It includes an overview of the SSI program, information on the SSI resource limits, and a discussion of how the marriage of an SSI beneficiary to either another beneficiary or an ineligible person can affect his or her eligibility for benefits or monthly benefit level. In some cases, marriage may result in a person being denied SSI benefits or having his or her monthly SSI benefit level reduced. This situation has been called a "marriage penalty" by the National Council on Disability.[1]

SUPPLEMENTAL SECURITY INCOME (SSI)

Under the provisions of Title XVI of the Social Security Act, disabled individuals and persons who are 65 or older are entitled to benefits from the SSI program if they have income and assets that fall below program guidelines. SSI benefits are paid out of the general revenue of the United States and all participants receive the same basic monthly federal benefit. In most states, adults who collect SSI are automatically entitled to coverage under the Medicaid health insurance program.[2]

The basic monthly federal benefit amount for 2007 is $623 for a single person and $934 for a couple. This amount is supplemented by 44 states and the District of Columbia. Arizona, Georgia, Kansas, Mississippi, Tennessee, West Virginia, and the Commonwealth of the Northern Mariana Islands do not offer a state supplement.[3]

A participant in the SSI program receives the federal benefit amount, plus any state supplement, minus any countable income.[4]

Table 1. Marital Status of U.S. Adult Population and SSI Adult Recipients by Age (in percent)

	Over Age 18		Age 18-64		Over Age 65	
	U.S.	SSI	U.S.	SSI	U.S	SSI
Married	54.1	22.4	54.0	20.4	54.3	26.3
Widowed	6.4	20.2	1.8	7.5	30.1	43.9
Divorced or Separated	15.5	26.9	21.3	29.9	11.8	21.0
Never Married	24.0	30.6	27.9	42.2	3.9	8.7

Source: Congressional Research Service (CRS) table with data on U.S. population taken from the United States Census Bureau 2005 American Community Survey and data on SSI taken from Social Security Administration, *SSI Annual Statistical Report, 2004* (Washington: GPO, 2005), Table 35.

Notes: Data on SSI is from the end of 2001. Numbers may not add up due to rounding. For additional information on the American Community Survey see the website of the United State Census Bureau at [http://www.census.gov/acs/www/index.html].

At the end of February 2007, nearly 7.3 million people received SSI benefits. In that month, these SSI beneficiaries each received an average federal cash benefit of $465.60 and the program paid out a total of over $3.5 billion in SSI benefits.[5] The average monthly benefit is lower than the federal benefit amount because a person's total monthly benefit may be lowered based on earnings and other income.

Nearly 70% of adult SSI recipients have been married at some point in their lives. Table 1 details the marital status of SSI recipients as compared to the overall population of the United States.

SSI Resource Limits

Individuals and couples must have limited assets or resources in order to qualify for SSI benefits.[6] Resources are defined by regulation as "cash or other liquid assets or any real or personal property that an individual (or spouse, if any) owns and could convert to cash to be used for his or her support and maintenance."[7] When a couple marries and pools their assets, they may find themselves with resources that render them ineligible for continued SSI benefits.

The countable resource limit for SSI eligibility is $2,000 for individuals and $3,000 for couples. These limits are set by law, are not indexed for inflation and have been at their current levels since 1989.[8] Not all resources are counted for SSI purposes. Excluded resources include an individual's home, a single car used for essential transportation and other assets specified by law and regulation.[9]

Potential Impact of Marriage on SSI Eligibility and Benefits

Marriage as Defined by the SSI Program

Federal regulations establish the definition of marriage for the purposes of determining SSI eligibility and calculating SSI benefits.[10] Two people are considered married for the purposes of the SSI program if one of the following conditions is present:

- The couple is legally married under the laws of the state in which they make their permanent home;
- The SSA has determined that either person is entitled to Social Security benefits as the spouse of the other person;[11] or
- The couple is living together in the same household and is leading people to believe that they are married.

Under the terms of the Defense of Marriage Act, P.L. 104-199, a married couple must consist of one man and one woman for the purposes of the SSI program.[12]

Marriage of an SSI Beneficiary to Another SSI Beneficiary

When two SSI beneficiaries marry, they are considered a beneficiary couple. As a result, they are entitled to a federal benefit of up to $904 per month and may have countable resources valued at up to $3,000. Their combined countable income is used to reduce their monthly benefit.

The marriage of two SSI beneficiaries can have a negative effect on their eligibility for benefits and their total amount of benefits. As a married couple, both beneficiaries are presumed to have access to the couple's shared income and resources. Compared with two single beneficiaries as single persons, a married couple has a lower resource limit, a lower maximum federal benefit, and a lower amount of excluded income as shown in table 2.

Table 2. Illustrative Comparison of SSI Income Exclusions and Benefits for Two Single Beneficiaries and a Married Couple

	Two Single Beneficiaries		Married Couple
	Man	Woman	
Monthly earned income	$200	$200	$400
Monthly maximum federal benefit	$603	$603	$904
Basic income exclusion	$85	$85	$85
Additional income exclusion (½ of earnings above $85)	$57.50	$57.50	$157.50
Countable income (earned income minus exclusions)	$57.50	$57.50	$157.50
Total monthly SSI benefit	$545.50	$545.50	$746.50
(Maximum federal benefit minus countable income)			
Combined monthly benefits		$1,091	$746.50

Source: Congressional Research Service (CRS).

Resource Limitations

Single SSI beneficiaries can have countable resources valued at up to $2,000. Combined, two such single beneficiaries can have a total of up to $4,000 in countable resources and can exclude from their countable resources two cars and two houses. However, as a married couple, their maximum amount of resources is $3,000 and they may exclude from their countable resources one car and one house.

Maximum Federal Benefit

The maximum federal SSI benefit for 2006 is $603 per month for a single beneficiary and $904 per month for a married couple. Two unmarried beneficiaries could each receive up to $603 per month in benefits or a combined monthly benefit of up to $1,206. However, as a married couple, these beneficiaries can receive a maximum benefit of $904 per month.

Income Exclusions

A single SSI beneficiary is allowed to exclude $85 of income (the first $20 in monthly earnings and $65 in earned income on top of the first $20) as well as one-half of all earned income above $65 from the income used to reduce the monthly SSI benefit. Two single beneficiaries can each exclude the basic $85 for a combined exclusion of $170. However, a married couple is entitled to exclude only the basic $85 and one-half of their combined earnings over $65.

MARRIAGE OF AN SSI BENEFICIARY TO A NON-BENEFICIARY

The marriage of an SSI beneficiary to a person who does not receive SSI benefits can have a negative effect on the SSI beneficiary's eligibility and amount of benefits if the ineligible spouse brings significant income or assets to the family. Generally, the income and assets of both persons in a marriage are considered shared and equally available to either person, which can result in an increase in the beneficiary's countable income or resources after marriage.

Deeming of Income

When an SSI beneficiary marries a person who does not receive SSI benefits, a portion of the ineligible spouse's income is assigned, or deemed, to the SSI beneficiary and is counted as income for the purposes of determining benefit eligibility and the amount of monthly benefits. The procedure used to deem income from an ineligible person to his or her spouse who receives SSI benefits consists of several steps set by regulation and takes into account the overall size of the family.[13] The four steps in the income deeming process are included below and two examples of income deeming are provided in table 3 at the end of this article.

Step 1. Determining the Countable Income of the Ineligible Spouse

The first step in the deeming process is to determine the countable monthly income of the ineligible spouse by taking his or her total earned and unearned income and reducing it by a special limited set of income exclusions. Generally, most income other than federal social service benefits is counted.[14]

Step 2. Allocating Income for Ineligible Children and Sponsored Aliens

Once the countable income of the ineligible spouse has been established, this amount is further reduced to account for any ineligible children living in the household or any aliens that the ineligible spouse may be sponsoring.[15] For each child or sponsored alien, the countable income of the ineligible spouse is reduced by an amount equal to the difference between the monthly federal SSI benefit rate for a couple and the monthly federal SSI benefit rate for an individual.[16] For 2007, this amount is $311, the difference between the federal SSI benefit rate for a couple of $934 and the rate for an individual of $623.

Step 3. Determining SSI Eligibility

The final countable monthly income of the ineligible spouse is used to determine the continued SSI eligibility of the beneficiary. If the final countable income of the ineligible spouse is less than or equal to the difference between the monthly federal SSI benefit rate for a couple and the monthly federal SSI benefit rate for an individual ($311 for 2007), then no income is deemed to the beneficiary and the beneficiary is eligible to continue receiving SSI benefits as an individual.

If, however, the final countable income of the ineligible spouse is greater than the difference between the monthly federal SSI benefit rate for a couple and the monthly federal SSI benefit rate for an individual, then the beneficiary and his or her spouse are considered a couple and eligible to receive SSI benefits at the level for a couple.

Step 4. Determining the SSI Benefit

If a married beneficiary is considered an individual after Step 3, then his or her monthly SSI benefit is equal to the federal benefit rate for an individual minus any of his or her countable income. The income of the ineligible spouse is not considered when determining the benefit amount in this case.

If, however, the married beneficiary and his or her spouse are considered a couple after Step 3, then their benefit is reduced by their combined countable income. The final countable income of the ineligible spouse is added to the total income of the beneficiary. This amount is then reduced by the standard income exclusions and the couple's monthly benefit is reduced by this final income amount.

Deeming of Resources

Unlike the rules governing the deeming of income from an ineligible spouse to an SSI beneficiary, the resource deeming rules are straightforward. Any resources owned by the ineligible spouse are deemed to the beneficiary. All of the resources of a married couple are considered to be available to the SSI beneficiary and are subject to the regular SSI resource limitations. If the beneficiary is considered a single beneficiary, then he or she may have countable resources valued at up to $2,000. If, after the deeming of income, he or she is considered part of a beneficiary couple, then the countable resource limit is $3,000. The only exception to this rule is that the pension plan of an ineligible spouse is not deemed to a beneficiary.

LEGISLATION INTRODUCED IN THE 110TH CONGRESS TO CHANGE THE WAY MARRIAGE AFFECTS THE SSI PROGRAM

To date, there have been no bills introduced in the 110th Congress that would directly change the way the marriage of an SSI beneficiary, either to another beneficiary or to a non-beneficiary, would affect the SSI eligibility and benefits of that beneficiary.

Table 3. Examples of Income Deeming When an SSI Beneficiary Marries an Ineligible Spouse

	Example 1		Example 2		
Monthly income of beneficiary		$0			$0
Monthly income of ineligible spouse		$800			$2,000
Step 1. Countable income of ineligible spouse		$800			$2,000
Step 2. Allocations for two children	Countable income	$800	Countable income		$2,000
	Minus allocations of $311 for each child	$622	Minus allocations of $311 for each child		$622
	Final countable income	$178	Final countable income		$1,378
Step 3. Eligibility determination	Final countable income of $198 is LESS THAN $311 so beneficiary is treated as an INDIVIDUAL		Final countable income of $1,398 is MORE THAN $311 so beneficiary is treated as a COUPLE		

Table 3. (Continued)

	Example 1		Example 2		
Step 4. Monthly benefit determination	Federal benefit for individual	$623	Federal benefit for couple		$934
	Minus countable income of beneficiary	$0	Minus countable income of couple	Income of beneficiary	$0
				Plus final countable income of ineligible spouse	$1,398
				Minus exclusions ($20, first $65 of all earned income, ½ of earned income above $65)	$741.50
				Couple's total countable income	$656.50
	Total monthly SSI benefit	$623	Total monthly SSI benefit		($934-$656.5) = $277.50
Combined monthly income and SSI benefit		*$1,423*			*$2,277.50*

Source: Congressional Research Service (CRS).

REFERENCES

[1] National Council on Disability, The Social Security Administration's Efforts to Promote Employment for People with Disabilities: New Solutions for Old Problems (Washington: GPO, 2005), pp. 62-64.

[2] Thirty-nine states, the District of Columbia, and the Commonwealth of the Northern Mariana Islands grant Medicaid eligibility to all adult SSI recipients, or have Medicaid eligibility rules that are the same as those of the SSI program. For more information, see [http://www.ssa.gov/work/ResourcesToolkit/Health/medicaid.html].

[3] SSI benefits are not available to residents of Puerto Rico, Guam, or the United States Virgin Islands. Residents of these jurisdictions are eligible to receive federal benefits from their commonwealth or territorial government under provisions of Title XIV and Title XVI of the Social Security Act. These benefits are administered by the Department of Health and Human Services.

[4] The first $20 of income in a month, the first $65 of earned income in a month, and one half of earned income above $65 in a month are not counted for the purposes of determining the SSI benefit level. For additional information on the SSI income rules, see CRS Report RS20294, SSI Income and Resource Limits: A Fact Sheet, by Scott Szymendera (hereafter cited as CRS Report RS20294).

[5] Social Security Administration, SSI Monthly Statistics, February 2006, table 1. Available on the website of the Social Security Administration at [http://www.ssa.gov/policy/docs/ statcomps/ssi_monthly/2007-02/table01.pdf].

[6] For additional information on the SSI resource rules, see CRS Report RS20294.

[7] 20 CFR § 416.1201.

[8] 42 USC § 1382(a).

[9] A complete list of excluded resources can be found at 20 CFR §§ 416.1210- 416.1247.

[10] 20 CFR § 416.1806.

[11] For additional information on husband's and wife's benefits, see CRS Report RS22294, Social Security Survivors Benefits, by Kathleen Romig and Scott Szymendera.

[12] For additional information on the Defense of Marriage Act and its application to Social Security programs, see CRS Report RL31994, Same Sex Marriage: Legal Issues, by Alison M. Smith and CRS Report RS21897, The Effect of State-Legalized Same Sex Marriage on Social Security Benefits and Pensions, by Laura Haltzel and Patrick Purcell.

[13] 20 CFR § 416.1163.

[14] A complete list of exclusions can be found at 20 CFR § 416.1161.

[15] Children who are receiving SSI or other public income maintenance payments are not counted.

[16] This amount is reduced by the amount of any income of the child or sponsored alien.

In: Families: Rights, Laws and Stability ISBN: 978-1-60456-203-3
Editors: J. R. Redmund, K. B. Killigan, pp. 129-135

Chapter 8

CHILD CUSTODY PROCEEDINGS UNDER THE INDIAN CHILD WELFARE ACT: AN OVERVIEW*

Kamilah M. Holder

ABSTRACT

In 1978, Congress enacted the Indian Child Welfare Act (ICWA) in response to legislative findings of harm caused to Indian children, their families, and tribes by the high separation rate of Indian children from their homes and cultural environments. Congress addressed this situation by granting Indian tribes and Indian parents an enhanced role in determining when to remove Indian children from their homes and cultural environments. Specifically, the ICWA enumerates provisions for tribal jurisdiction and tribal intervention in state court proceedings concerning the custody, adoption, foster care placement, and termination of parental rights of Indian children.

No bills amending the ICWA were introduced in the 109th Congress. Still, the debate over provisions of the ICWA remains an issue of concern. This CRS report provides an overview of some of the goals and provisions of the Indian Child Welfare Act.

BACKGROUND

Congress enacted the Indian Child Welfare Act (ICWA)[1] in 1978 to address the high rate of separation of Indian children from their homes and cultural environments.[2] Prior to 1978, as many as 25 to 35 percent of the Indian children in some states were removed from their homes and placed in non-Indian homes.[3] This practice of removal fragmented families and threatened the continued survival of Native American tribes. Respect for the self-determination of tribes required, in the view of Congress, that tribes be given a greater say in decisions affecting Indian children.[4] In evaluating the perceived biases of state agencies, the

* Excerpted from CRS Report RS22554, dated December 14, 2006.

House report accompanying the legislation cited the apparent inability of social workers to accord proper recognition to factors in Indian environments that tended to mitigate the severe economic deprivations found on many reservations, deprivations that often served as a basis for state agency neglect findings.[5] The legislative history also indicated that Indian parents often lacked adequate legal representation in child custody proceedings and were frequently coerced into voluntary waivers of their parental rights.[6] As a result, addressing the situation was thought to require both procedural and substantive components to promote a policy of stability and security for Indian tribes and families while also ensuring that the foster and adoptive homes of Indian children reflected the unique values of Indian culture.[7]

COVERAGE

The ICWA applies to Indian children involved in certain child custody proceedings. For purposes of the ICWA, an Indian child is an unmarried individual under age 18 who is either a member of a federally recognized Indian tribe or the biological child of a member of a tribe and eligible for membership in a tribe.[8] Membership eligibility is evaluated by tribes and the requirements vary widely by tribe.[9] Under the ICWA, Indian custodians include any Indian person with legal custody of an Indian child under tribal laws, customs, state laws or "to whom temporary physical care, custody, and control has been transferred by the parent of such child."[10] The ICWA applies in the following child custody proceedings:

- a foster care placement;[11]
- any action "resulting in the termination of the parent-child relationship";[12]
- a pre-adoptive placement that consists of "the temporary placement of an Indian child in a foster home or institution after the termination of parental rights but prior to or in lieu of adoptive placement;"[13] and
- an adoptive placement, which refers to the final placement of an Indian child for adoption including any action that results in a final decree of adoption.[14]

However, "child custody proceeding" does not include an award of custody in a divorce proceeding; nor does it include a placement based upon an action by the child that would be a crime if committed by an adult.[15]

JURISDICTION

Among the most important elements of the ICWA are its jurisdictional provisions. In enacting the ICWA, Congress recognized that Indian tribes have distinct societal interests in the lives of Indian children that can be distinguished from that of the parents. In preserving these interests, the ICWA both enhances the jurisdictional reach of tribal courts and provides a right of intervention in state court proceedings that involve Indian children.[16] In part, the act delineates areas of exclusive tribal jurisdiction and those of concurrent state and tribal jurisdiction.

Exclusive Tribal Jurisdiction

Under the ICWA, an Indian tribe generally has exclusive jurisdiction over an Indian child who resides or is domiciled within the tribe's land.[17] Indian tribes also have exclusive jurisdiction over Indian children who are wards of a tribal court that has previously exercised jurisdiction over their cases.[18] There are two exceptions to the grant of exclusive tribal jurisdiction. Tribal courts do not have jurisdiction where jurisdiction is "otherwise vested in the State by existing Federal law."[19] The other exception is the emergency removal of a child who resides or "is domiciled on the reservation, but temporarily located off the reservation, from his parent or Indian guardian in order to prevent imminent physical harm."[20] Under the ICWA, federal, state and tribal courts must all afford full faith and credit to the orders and judgments of a tribal court that has exercised jurisdiction in an Indian child custody proceeding.[21]

Concurrent Jurisdiction

In child custody proceedings involving Indian children not residing or domiciled on the tribe's land, the ICWA confers concurrent jurisdiction on tribal and state courts.[22] The ICWA expresses a preference for tribal jurisdiction in child custody proceedings involving Indian children. As such, state court proceedings that address foster care placement or termination of parental rights and involve Indian children residing or domiciled off the reservation may be transferred to tribal courts. This transfer shall take place upon the petition of either parent, the Indian custodian or the child's tribe unless one of the child's parents objects, the tribal court declines jurisdiction or good cause to deny transfer exists.[23] The first two exceptions present very little room for judicial analysis; however, the "good cause" exception is a broader area of judicial interpretation. Guidelines, issued by the Department of the Interior, state that a party opposing transfer to a tribal court bears the burden of demonstrating good cause to deny transfer.[24] The Guidelines also provide examples of what constitutes good cause.[25]

Judicial Decisions

The only U.S. Supreme Court case to address the ICWA dealt with the statutory construction of the act's domicile provision and how it was to be interpreted. In *Mississippi Band of Choctaw Indians v. Holyfield*, the Supreme Court determined that for purposes of the ICWA a child's domicile at birth is that of his or her parents at the time of birth.[26] In reaching this decision, the Court reasoned that the purpose of the statute indicated congressional intent to establish uniformity in the application of the ICWA, instead of allowing varied state court definitions of a key term to dictate ICWA application. Thus, the Court held that an Indian tribe had jurisdiction over twin baby girls whose parents took care to have the children born off the reservation in order to put the children up for adoption under state law.

State courts have developed different approaches to addressing general questions of ICWA applicability and such other concerns as the grounds for invoking the "good cause" exception to transfer. For example, some state court judicial decisions scrutinize the level of contact between an Indian child and the Indian tribe or reservation, while other courts engage in a "best interests of the child" analysis in assessing possible reasons for transfer.[27] Other courts have dealt with the issue of applying the judicially crafted "existing Indian family exception" with varying results.[28]

Procedural Protections in State Courts

In expanding the ability of tribes to strengthen and preserve Indian families, the ICWA not only enhances tribal jurisdiction but also provides comprehensive procedural protections for Indian tribes, parents and custodians throughout state court proceedings. For example, where a state court knows or has reason to know at the outset of an involuntary custody proceeding that the child at issue is an Indian child, the ICWA requires that the party seeking termination of parental rights or foster care placement notify the child's parent or Indian custodian and tribe.[29] Notice must be given at least ten days before the advancement of the state proceedings.[30] Tribes must be notified of their unconditional right to intervene in the state court proceeding and their right to examine all relevant documents as well as their ability to obtain a delay of the proceedings.[31] These provisions are all aimed at ensuring that parents, custodians and tribes are aware of their rights under the ICWA and are given adequate time to exercise these rights.

Additional provisions, applicable in both voluntary and involuntary cases, are also intended to ensure that Indian parents, custodians and tribes are not misled or coerced into losing their rights to rear Indian children. As such, cases that proceed in state courts are subject to a number of procedural protections, whether the proceeding is voluntary or involuntary. Voluntary proceedings consist of tribal member parents choosing termination of parental rights and adoption or foster care placement of their child. Involuntary proceedings involve state attempts to terminate parental rights or place Indian children in foster care. Tribes may intervene in both involuntary and voluntary proceedings. Also, an Indian child's tribe, parent, Indian custodian or an "Indian child who is the subject of an action for foster care placement or termination of parental rights under state law" may seek to invalidate the action upon a showing that the action violated provisions of the ICWA.[32]

Voluntary Proceedings

For any voluntary placement to be valid, the consent of the Indian parent must be in writing and executed before a judge of a court of appropriate jurisdiction. The judge must certify that the consequences of the action to be undertaken are explained to the parent in a language that the parent understands. The consent to the termination of parental rights cannot be executed until after the child is 10 days old.[33] Indian parents can revoke their consent at any time during their child's foster care placement or before a decree of termination or adoption has been entered.[34] Upon revoking consent, the parent would be entitled to the immediate return of the child. However, in cases of adoption where an order accepting the voluntary termination of parental rights has been entered, then the parent may not revoke consent.

Involuntary Proceedings

First, the party seeking foster care placement or the termination of parental rights must provide notice of the proceedings to the parent or Indian custodian and the child's tribe.[35] The ICWA gives indigent parents or Indian custodians the right to court-appointed counsel in any involuntary removal, placement or termination proceeding.[36] In involuntary proceedings, the parties also have the right to examine all reports or other documents filed with the court on which any decision may be based.[37] Furthermore, a state court cannot order an involuntary foster care placement unless it determines that the parent's or Indian custodian's continued custody of the child is likely to result in serious emotional or physical damage to the child.[38] The determination must also meet the clear and convincing standard and be based on evidence that includes testimony from at least one qualified expert witness.[39] In order to terminate parental rights or initiate foster care placement in regard to an Indian child, a state court must ensure that active efforts have been taken to provide remedial services and rehabilitative programs to Indian parents and custodians in order to prevent the breakup of the Indian family.[40]

ADOPTIVE PLACEMENTS

The ICWA also addresses adoption. The ICWA establishes an order of preference for adoptive placement of an Indian child under state law, "in the absence of good cause to the contrary," that looks to placing a child with extended family members, other members of the tribe or Indian families.[41] Also, the ICWA establishes a placement preference plan to be followed in foster care and preadoptive placements.[42] Tribes may establish a different order of preference by resolution, to be followed in the aforementioned placements.[43]

PROPOSED LEGISLATION

Although there have been attempts to amend the ICWA in earlier Congresses,[44] no legislative proposals to amend the Indian Child Welfare Act were introduced in the 109th Congress.

REFERENCES

[1] P.L. 95-608, 92 Stat. 3069 (1978); codified at 25 U.S.C. §§ 1901 -1963.
[2] 25 U.S.C. § 1901(4). This embodies a congressional finding that an alarmingly high number of Indian children were being removed from their homes by nontribal public and private agencies and often placed in non-Indian institutions or homes.
[3] H.Rept. 95-1386, 95th Cong., 2d Sess. 9 (1978).
[4] Id.
[5] Id.
[6] Id.
[7] 25 U.S.C. § 1902.

[8] 25 U.S.C. § 1903(4). Under 25 U.S.C. § 1903(8), " 'Indian tribe' means any Indian tribe, band, nation or other organized group or community of Indians recognized as eligible for the services provided to Indians by the Secretary of the Interior because of their status as Indians, including any Alaska Native village as defined in section 1602(c) of Title 43."

[9] Cohen's Handbook of Federal Indian Law § 3.03[2] (Nell Jessup Newton et al. eds., 2005 ed.) [hereinafter Cohen's Handbook].

[10] 25 U.S.C. § 1903(6).

[11] 25 U.S.C. § 1903(1)(i). "Foster care placement" encompasses placements in which the parent or Indian custodian cannot have the child returned upon demand but the parent's rights have not been terminated.

[12] 25 U.S.C. § 1903(1)(ii).

[13] 25 U.S.C. § 1903(1)(iii).

[14] 25 U.S.C. § 1903(1)(iv).

[15] 25 U.S.C. § 1903(1).

[16] 25 U.S.C. § 1903(12) defines tribal court as "a court with jurisdiction over child custody proceedings and which is either a Court of Indian Offenses, a court established and operated under the code or custom of an Indian tribe, or any other administrative body of a tribe which is vested with authority over child custody proceedings."

[17] 25 U.S.C. § 1911(a).

[18] Id.

[19] 25 U.S.C. § 1911(a). This exception most often applies in states that have assumed civil jurisdiction over Indian reservations under laws such as Public Law 280 (25 U.S.C. §1321-25). (Public Law 280 is the popular name of P.L. 83-280, as amended, a law conferring jurisdiction over activities in most of the Indian country in specified states to state courts.) However, in these circumstances, 25 U.S.C. §1918 authorizes tribes to retake jurisdiction over child custody proceedings upon approval by the Secretary of the Interior.

[20] 25 U.S.C. § 1922.

[21] 25 U.S.C. § 1911(d).

[22] 25 U.S.C. § 1911(b).

[23] 25 U.S.C. § 1911(b).

[24] Guidelines for State Courts; Indian Child Custody Proceedings, 44 Fed. Reg. 67,584 (Nov. 29, 1979).

[25] *See* id. at 67,591 (Guideline C.3(b)(i) and (iii)).

[26] 490 U.S. 30 (1989).

[27] Cohen's Handbook § 11.03.

[28] *Compare, e.g., In re Adoption of Baby Boy L,* 643 P.2d 168 (Kan. 1982) (court did not apply provisions of ICWA over the objections of a child's Indian father and his tribe after finding that the child had no ties to his Indian father or the tribe and was not part of an existing Indian family) *and In re Baby Boy C,* 805 N.Y.S.2d 313, 27 A.D.3d 34 (N.Y. 2005) (court declined to adopt the "existing Indian family exception" on the grounds that it was inconsistent with the provisions of the ICWA).

[29] 25 U.S.C. § 1912(a).

[30] Id.

[31] Id.

[32] 25 U.S.C. § 1914.
[33] 25 U.S.C. § 1913(a).
[34] 25 U.S.C. § 1913(b).
[35] 25 U.S.C. § 1912(a).
[36] 25 U.S.C. § 1912(b).
[37] 25 U.S.C. § 1912(c).
[38] 25 U.S.C. § 1912(e).
[39] 25 U.S.C. § 1912(f).
[40] 25 U.S.C. § 1912(d).
[41] 25 U.S.C. § 1915(a).
[42] 25 U.S.C. § 1915(b).
[43] 25 U.S.C. § 1915(c).
[44] Marcie Yablon, *The Indian Child Welfare Act Amendments of 2003*, 38 Fam. L.Q. 689 (2004-2005) (discussing proposals to, *e.g,* address judicial decisions that put certain children beyond he reach of the ICWA because they were not part of an "existing Indian family").

INDEX

A

B

C

G

H